# FOR EVERYONE A GARDEN

The MIT Press

Cambridge, Massachusetts,

and London, England

# FOR EVERYONE A GARDEN

Moshe Safdie

Edited by Judith Wolin

This book was designed and produced by
The MIT Press Media Department.

It was set in IBM Composer Univers,
printed on Mead Moistrite Matte
by Eastern Press, Inc.,
and bound in G.S.B. S/535/83 "Lime"
by Robert Burlen & Son, Inc.,
in the United States of America.

Library of Congress Cataloging in Publication Data

Safdie, Moshe, 1938-
  For everyone a garden.

  1. Safdie, Moshe, 1938-        I. Title.
NA749.S2W64  720'.92'4  73-16432
ISBN 0-262-19108-3

For My Father and Mother

# CONTENTS

## ACKNOWLEDGMENTS

The projects illustrated in this book are the sum total of the efforts of ten years. They are the results of the intense effort by the individuals who make up my office. I want here to express my appreciation to those who have been in the past and who are presently members of this team.

Our work involves close collaboration with many specialist consultants who bear with us patiently, sometimes impatiently, in resolving the problems of our building efforts. To them too—much appreciation.

Thanks also to Judy Wolin, who is editor of this book and who reviewed all the material, structured and established the format, and assisted in editing and arranging the text. John Kettle, who edited Beyond Habitat, was most helpful in reviewing and rearranging the text for this book.

The book would not have been possible without a generous grant made by the Canada Council which enabled gathering and organizing the visual material, photographing the buildings, and preparing for publication.

Moshe Safdie

Moshe Safdie rarely sits still, much less stays in one city for more than two or three days at a time. The variety of his experiences and acquaintances is vast, and the number of large-scale projects that have come to his offices in Montreal and Jerusalem in the last decade has been unusual for so young a man. From all this "input" I might have expected to find some mighty garbled "output" in the form of projects of widely varying conviction and ambitions.

But what I found instead in him was a stubbornly consistent idealism. Every proposal expressed in some form Moshe's commitment to a more rationally organized and integrated urban structure; to a particular quality of scale for residential environments and a doggedly high standard of amenity for the individual dwelling.

In almost every way (with the major exception of his determination to master industrialized building techniques) Moshe is a very old-fashioned planner and architect, in the tradition of Frederick Law Olmsted or Frank Lloyd Wright. The sensual qualities of his spaces concern him very much; the natural landscape literally is woven through and over his structures, and the pedestrian is always secluded from vehicular traffic.

He has become stereotyped, I think, as a man obsessed with repetitive geometric volumes arranged in pyramidal piles. But I think Moshe sees repetitive building elements—his "toys"—as the way to get where he wants to go. A basic building element big enough, and complex enough to achieve the grand public spaces of his three-dimensional city; and full of facets to capture changing light and view. At every opportunity, he tries out new modular shapes and new ways to connect them. Sometimes, in spite of advantageous structural properties or intriguing space-use possibilities, they simply do not work. But no "failures" have been edited out of this book, because in spite of their problems, they reveal the constant energy that he invests in the search for a spatial structure that will do something more than "pack well."

I would like to offer one piece of unsolicited advice to the reader. The temptation to become preoccupied with the individual elements of which the structure is composed is very strong; but that would be like becoming fascinated with the bricks of a house and ignoring the edifice. The essence of Moshe Safdie's work is in the many surfaces that he exposes to the sun, rain, and wind, and in the quality and generosity of the spaces that are left "unpacked."

J. W.

# FOR EVERYONE A GARDEN

# 1

## THE THREE-DIMENSIONAL COMMUNITY

When in Japan in 1970, I visited the offices of several of the "Metabolist" architects. I went there with the conviction that they were in the forefront of thinking about the three-dimensional city. Just emerging from the struggle to get Puerto Rico Habitat under way, I was quite conscious of the problems of making a complex structure work at the mundane level of building codes, plumbing systems, circulation, and economic constraints. The questions I asked the Japanese had to do with problems such as What kind of structure could possibly hold their buildings up, or How could someone move around inside of them, or What materials would be used? Often the response was that this had not yet been considered. The implication was that their studies were theoretical and my questions were therefore irrelevant. The question is, How much impact does this theoretical work have on the world we actually have to live in? What we see being built instead are those dismal and vast housing projects that ring Tokyo, Paris, Rome, and Moscow. We may dislike what the Russians are building in Moscow, but it's foolish simply to dismiss it all, as professional critics do; these suburbs are, in fact, a realistic expression of what our present system for building housing is able to produce.

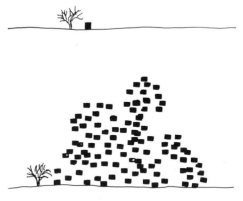

When I first looked at cities, it was in terms of organizational structure. I went through a simple exercise. I listed general categories of functions that go on in a city and then the estimated volume of space each occupied into imaginary cubes, coding each cube according to its function. Color was used to express functional characteristics, such as need for daylight. I then drew cross sections of several central city areas using this notation. The resulting diagram of down-town Philadelphia or Montreal is a totally irrational pattern. Town houses are in the shadow of parking structures, parks in the shadow of office buildings.

A diagram of circulation patterns in an area where four or five tall buildings are side by side might sometimes show substantial movement between various offices on their upper levels. But you know that everyone must go down to street level, where the cars move, and cross the traffic to get to the next build-

ing. Underground pedestrian passages, like the ones in Montreal, don't overcome the need to go twenty stories down and then twenty stories up again to make that kind of communication. And the people move in tunnels underground, while the cars move in the sunlight overhead!

We could instead consider the optimum movement system as a three-dimensional lattice. What if pedestrians could move about at a level ten stories in the air? If instead of what we call an "elevator," vertical movement becomes a form of public mass transit? If elevators become, instead, horizontal and diagonal conveyors? We take for granted the feasibility of a thousand-foot-high building with dozens of elevators, but putting this same building on its side and serving it from one access point with a thousand-foot-long horizontal conveyor (which is much cheaper) sounds like a fantasy. But, in fact, we could build mountain slopes of houses. We could plan for optimum orientation. The valleys would be parks; within the hollow mountain would be public spaces, with shops, theaters, and other public facilities. The slopes of the houses would be membrances, lacelike in their openness, admitting light, yet giving shelter to the public spaces.

So with these thoughts as a starting point—"intentions" might be a better word—I put together a plan for a city with two hundred thousand inhabitants. I wanted to demonstrate that the city could be built at a population density comparable with the downtown areas of Montreal or Boston without compromising the quality of environment of each particular urban activity, whether it was shopping, or housing, or work. I also wanted to show that an inhabitant of this city could have complete mobility without owning an automobile, yet without ever having to walk more than a thousand feet.

The site chosen was Giza. I had some rather naïve ideas in 1962 about the possibility of resettling Palestinian refugees in a new model city that would be funded by the world community through the United Nations, the compensation money forthcoming from Israel. I also thought that a sophisticated industrialized building facility could provide a future economic base for the city. The idea of model communities for the refugees was right, but the proposed solution was more appropriate to the industrialized areas of Japan, the United States, and Western Europe.

In the Giza plan I proposed a whole series of synchronized movement systems that formed a network around the Sphinx and the Pyramids. They ranged from moving sidewalks and escalators to a high-speed train linking the city with metropolitan Cairo. Housing was accommodated in inclined membranes rising thirty levels in the air, sheltering the public spaces below.

Giza was obviously a theoretical study. It affirmed my conviction that there were more rational ways to organize urban life and the systems serving it than by simply building more and bigger roads, subdividing more land into little parcels, and accepting our present mode of "two-dimensional" planning as unalterable.

I came to believe that it might be possible to let a city grow the way a shell does, each increment of expansion proportionately greater than the previous one. For instance, in my sketches for a master plan for Tel Aviv, I applied this concept of "gnomonic" growth. In the first stage, a ten-story-high, three-dimensional structure provides for a certain proportion of residential, commercial, institutional, and park spaces. In the second phase, perhaps ten years later, a structure twice the height, but with the same proportional mix of facilities, can be erected; then the third stage, with an even greater density and height. What this assumes is that with each phase of development greater financial and technical means are available and greater density is necessary; so that the city, like an organism, builds at a progressively more ambitious scale as it acquires strength from its previous growth.

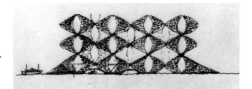

But I don't mean that one should just add more and more pieces to the pile. There must not only be small parks for each neighborhood but larger open spaces as well, and not only small neighborhood streets, ad infinitum, but larger and higher-speed systems of movement and larger commercial facilities.

It seems to me that we have learned to deal competently with the smallest-scale problems. The bathroom that I designed for Habitat 67 could have been designed just as well, if not better, by many other people who would put their minds to designing a good bathroom or even a good apartment. But I think as we move to the scale of Habitat itself, we are already involved in difficult problems of repetition and orientation, and when we start talking about communities of five thousand families such as the one I am working on for Baltimore or the new towns in the suburbs of Paris and London, it becomes obvious that we are quite ignorant about how to make them work.

The recent struggle to create a workable master plan for the city of Jerusalem points out how failures can occur. As a member of a committee asked to review the Jerusalem Master Plan, I was expected to give my opinion. Basically, I had little argument with the objectives. It stated that the city should be kept concentrated, and many open spaces should be left around it and should penetrate into the dense urban area. I agree with that. It stated that the city should have efficient mass transportation systems. But when you looked at the plan, you could see by the way the roads were proposed that the automobile had been given free rein. And there was nothing in the plan that could either halt or promote new developments on the surrounding hills or control their design. So the plan was really ineffective in determining the quality of the environment. It could set some general guidelines for density and open space but not for their quality.

The tool kit of the master planner needs to be expanded so that it includes not only general land-use maps and street patterns but explicit rules that set up criteria for, say, the orientation of dwelling units to the sun and view; the relationship of pedestrian movement or vehicular traffic; a certain minimum of private open space per unit; or the massing of buildings and their relation to the land. When work began on Expo in 1963, we were hoping that we could create this kind of master plan. Most of the designers involved were convinced that the idea of separate national pavilions was obsolete.

It seemed absurd that each nation would come and spend all that money competing for attention and have it all demolished a year later. The Montebello Conference, which was called to conceive Expo, suggested instead the idea of theme pavilions, which would deal with particular subjects, and to which several countries might contribute. For example, there might have been one about food and agriculture, another about education, another about medicine and health.

The very first Habitat proposal was to build a supercommunity, that is, a community at superscale. The complex would contain all the institutions of a city: schools, shopping, clinics, galleries, theaters. Each country or group of countries would build as its contribution a real school, a real theater. It would have been a situation analogous to that of the real city, with nations playing the role that developers and authorities normally do when they build within an urban infrastructure. At the end of Expo, a living community would have remained—one that we could have continued to learn from and enjoy.

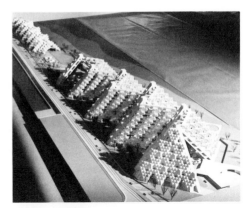

The Expo site was chosen to make the exhibition a permanent asset to the city; the mass transit lines, the parking facilities, the parks, the structures, the bridges and canals would remain as amenities even if their use changed. To reinforce this, I proposed to the city of Montreal, after Expo in 1968, that the Expo Islands be used for new housing, a new university, and other public facilities. There were many structures there, such as the U.S. Pavilion and the theme buildings, that could have continued to have vital uses. The housing development and transit lines could have extended to several of the St. Lawrence islands to the north. I called the plan Cité des Iles.

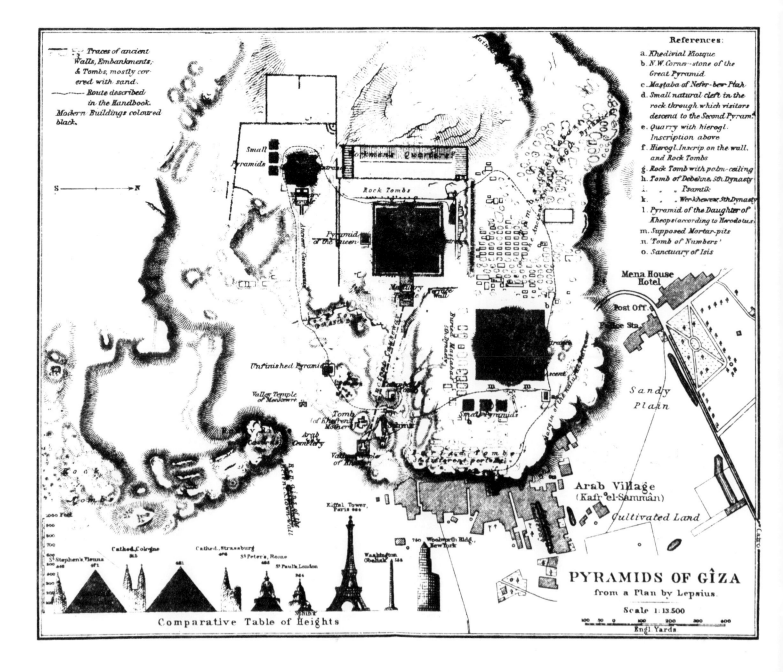

## Plan for the city of Giza

In 1962, I became very concerned and interested in the problems of the resettlement of the Arab refugees. This was several years after the Suez War, at a time when a suspended state of war existed in the Middle East. It seemed that a political solution was far off but that a social solution, based on a resettlement program, might remove some of the obstacles to an eventual total political settlement. In retrospect, I made certain naïve assumptions. One was that the governments of the Arab countries would accept resettlement in their own territory of a certain portion of the Palestinian refugees; another was that the Palestinians would accept resettlement on that basis.

The concept was to build an urban sector accommodating two hundred and fifty thousand people, located in the surrounds of the Pyramids of Giza and forming a natural urban extension of metropolitan Cairo. It brought together the various concepts I had been considering for the formation of a workable high-density environment, the three-dimensional reorganization of urban land uses, the organization of habitation as individual dwellings in a spatial grouping, the construction of a hierarchical public movement system that provided complete mobility without dependence on personal vehicles, and the utilization of mass-production construction techniques.

The idea was to construct a number of sophisticated housing factories and training centers. The refugees, who at the time were totally unemployed, were to be trained in building skills and to participate in the construction of their own environment (which would not be limited to refugee population). The factories would remain part of the industrial base of the new community, and the refugees might own these factories and the products of its construction cooperatively.

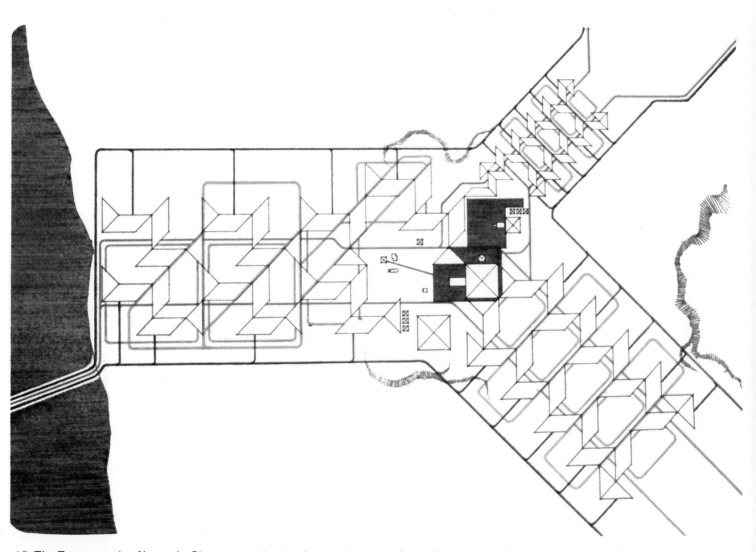

### 13. **The Transportation Network, Giza**

The continuous-motion transit principle is here applied at the scale of an urban sector. Systems of movement replacing conventional subways, buses, elevators, and sidewalks are integrated into a single hierarchical network of mass transit moving at accelerating and decelerating speeds ranging from 60 miles per hour to 2 miles per hour. Starting on a journey, one would embark on a moving sidewalk or vertical elevator that, rather than stop, would accelerate at certain intervals to greater speeds where one makes a transfer in motion to the second and faster system. If traveling a greater distance, one would then make another transfer when that system accelerates to meet the prime urban transit system, which again never comes to a stop, but rather accelerates and decelerates.

In this way complete mobility is achieved without ever having to walk more than a thousand feet and without ever having to resort to personal vehicles, yet without ever having to wait for the public transit system.

### 14. Land Use, Giza

Retail and commercial development, institutions, housing, and industry are integrated into a three-dimensional-space subdivision pattern achieving extremely high densities (two hundred persons per acre) without the sacrifices of the quality of environment.

Housing membranes form continuous networks sheltering public spaces with retail and institutional facilities. The three pyramids of Giza define the city center, and the major meeting space is designed surrounding the complex of the ancient palace and the Sphinx.

15-18. Sketches. New city of Giza.

19. Plan for the new city of Giza. View of the model showing the ancient Pyramids and Sphinx at the center of the complex.

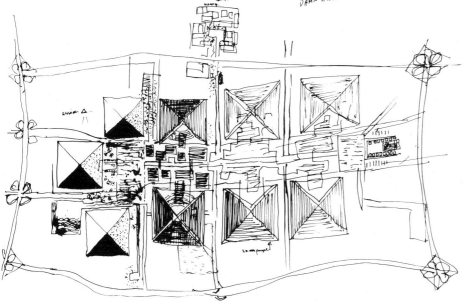

PROPOSED TOWN OF GIZA —
POP 200,000 FOR ARAB REFUGESE
FINANCED BY WORD BANK /
ISRAEL. UN. / ETC.
USA
INCLUDING SOME ARCH REMAINS OF ASUAN
DAMN AREA.

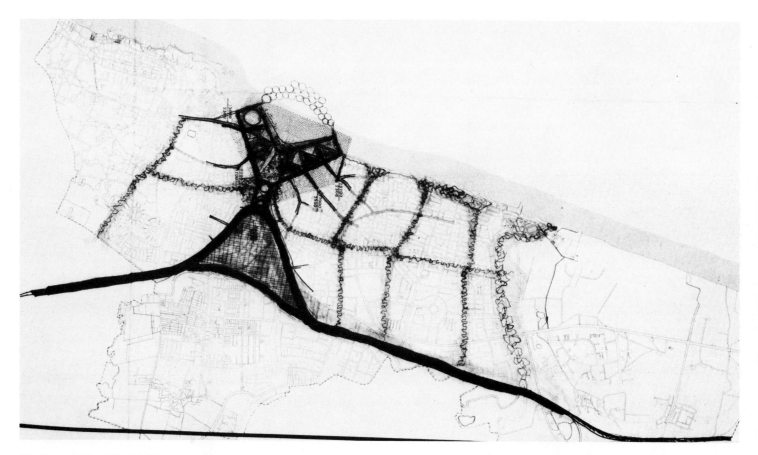

### 20. Competition for the Manchia area, Tel Aviv (1963)

A competition calling for proposals for the creation of a central business district in the area linking ancient Jaffa with modern Tel Aviv generated unexpected conclusions. First, that the center of Tel Aviv could not be viewed in the context of that city alone but was in fact a major cultural commercial center for the entire state of Israel.

Once transportation moving at speeds of 200 and 300 miles per hour is constructed (an inevitable development), Israel will become a single urban region all within 1-hour accessibility from any given point. The center of Manchia becomes a major facility serving the entire population. Manchia was therefore conceived as a highly accessible point on an urban transportation spine running from the northern cities to the port of Elat.

As a national center, the intensity of its construction would be substantial but must be conceived as an activity spanning at least fifty years. At any given point in time, the development must have a wholeness. The concept of gnomonic growth in progressive increments over a period of time (vividly seen in the growth of the Nautilus shell) is applied here.

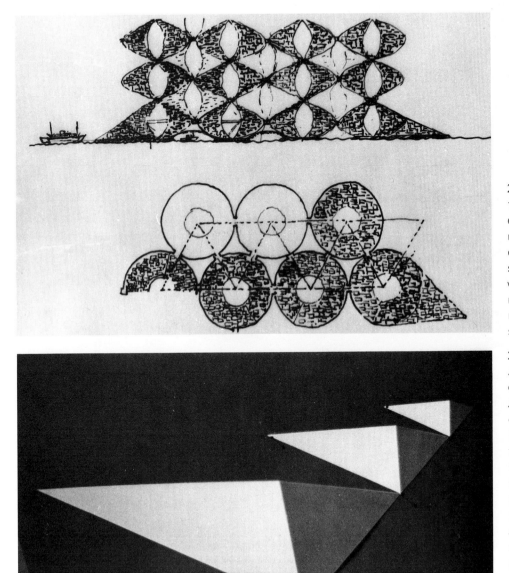

21. The program of the competition called for creating landfill along the seashore. Rather than building conventional structures over rock and mud placed in the sea, the scheme called for the construction of large helical structures that sat over foundations in the water itself. The helical pattern created a network of horizontal and inclined public movement paths that replaced the need for streets and passages on the ground.

22. **Gnomonic growth**
A diagrammatic pattern of development for each of the six sectors in the Manchia area. A three-dimensional network of housing, commercial, and institutional facilities (similar to the one illustrated in the Giza new town) is structured in a sequence of increasing density. In the first cycle, structures up to ten floors in height accommodate the variety of urban functions. As pressure on the land increases, in proportion to technical and financial resources of the country, the second phase, with double the density, is constructed. Subsequently, as both pressure and resources increase further, an urban structure rising 400 feet in height is constructed. Park space increases in proportion to the built-up urban space.

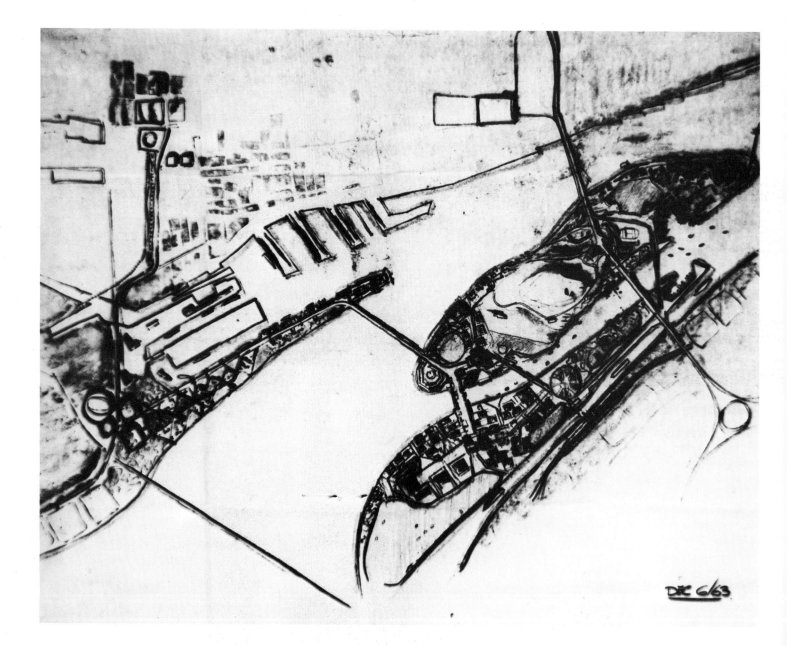

23. **The final sketch for the Expo Master Plan, prepared December 6, 1963**
This was the basic document from which the working master plan was prepared. A synchronized three-level transportation system that had been proposed earlier was not included, but a monorail train was maintained on the plan, with the major stations at the theme structures. The plan included a proposal for lakes and canals which were formed by the excavation of the rock that was needed to build the surrounding dykes.

24. **The Actual Expo Master Plan**
The official Expo Master Plan with the final arrangement of canals, lakes, pavilion locations, theme buildings, and the original plan for Habitat 67. McKay Pier was later renamed Cité du Havre and was replanned when Habitat was reduced in scale and various other pavilions were added.

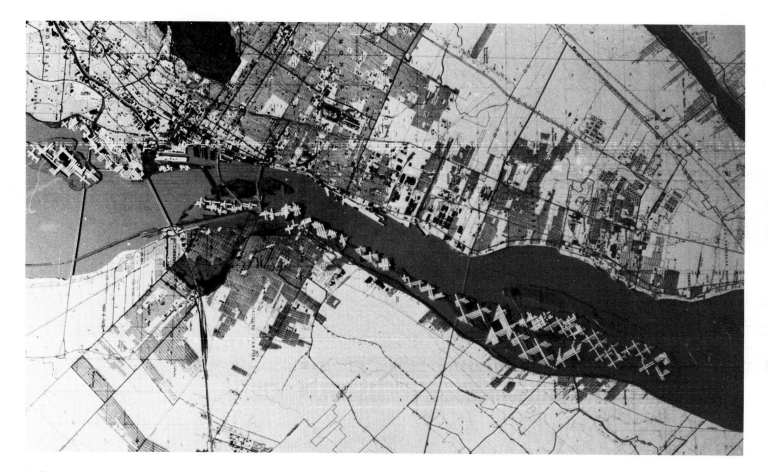

### Cité des Iles

The Cité des Iles Plan was a proposal made to the city of Montreal following the close of Expo. The generating idea behind Cité des Iles was to revitalize Expo by converting it from a temporary exhibit into a permanent part of the city proper and using all the infrastructure facilities and pavilions as a town center for a community of a quarter of a million people. All the islands south of

Expo in the St. Lawrence could be linked together into one linear city by an efficient mass transit system that could be an extension of the Expo express. Most of these islands are property of the National Harbours Board, that is, of the federal government, and therefore might more easily be developed in an integrated way. The islands are located in the geographic center of Montreal's east end industrial complex and be-

cause of the mass transit connection would be ten minutes from downtown Montreal. The plan was presented with the enthusiastic support of Colonel E. Churchill, the director of the installation of Expo, to Lucien Saulnier, chairman of the Executive Committee of the city of Montreal, and later on to Mayor Drapeau. The plan was well received. But Mayor Drapeau stated that, inasmuch as the islands are mostly located in neighboring

RESIDENTIAL
COMMERCIAL · RETAIL
EDUCATIONAL · CULTURAL
OFFICE · RESEARCH CTRE.
PARK

1 INTERNATIONAL RESEARCH CENTER
2 HIGH SCHOOL - QUEBEC PAV.
3
4 THEME BLDG · COMMUNITY CENTRE

CITÉ DES ÎLES - Proposal for Expo Islands

municipalities, it would be impossible for the city of Montreal to take the initiative in organizing such a plan. The provincial government and the federal government would have to initiate such an action jointly. The plan was also presented in 1968 to the federal minister in charge of urban affairs, Paul Hellier, through a meeting with the Task Force on Canadian Housing.

### 26. Cité des Iles
Proposal to Mayor Drapeau for revitalization of the Expo grounds. The proposal calls for retaining the canals, theme buildings, and some of the pavilions as community structures, shopping, and other public facilities, forming the nucleus of a town center for a community beginning with Nun's Island and Habitat and extending to the Expo site and southwards to the islands of the St. Law-

rence. Ile Notre Dame is to be rearranged with high-density housing along the existing canals, with Ile Verte remaining as a cultural recreational center.

AVANT GARDE

110 WEST 40TH STREET, NEW YORK, N.Y. 10018 · BR 9-1900

18 NOVEMBER 68

DEAR MR. SAFDIE,

IN 1976, LESS THAN A DECADE FROM NOW, THE UNITED STATES
WILL CELEBRATE ITS BICENTENNIAL. WE, THE EDITORS OF
AVANT-GARDE, ARE INVITING FIFTEEN OF THE WORLD'S MOST
DISTINGUISHED ARCHITECTS--YOURSELF INCLUDED--TO SEND
US SUGGESTIONS ON THE SHAPE AND FORM THAT THE CELEBRATION
OF AMERICA'S 200TH BIRTHDAY SHOULD TAKE. THAT IS,
WE WOULD APPRECIATE YOUR SENDING US (A) A STATEMENT
CONCERNING THE GENERAL PHILOSOPHY THAT SHOULD UNDERLIE
THE CELEBRATION, AND/OR (B) CONCRETE SUGGESTIONS
CONCERNING AN EXPOSITION, TYPES OF BUILDINGS, SITE,
MONUMENTS, ARCHITECTURAL INNOVATIONS, ETC.

THE STATEMENTS WILL BE PUBLISHED IN AVANT-GARDE IN
FEBRUARY, 1969, AND WE WOULD APPRECIATE RECEIVING
YOUR STATEMENT NOT LATER THAN JANUARY 6TH. YOU MAY
MAKE YOUR STATEMENT AS LONG OR AS SHORT AS YOU LIKE.
IF YOU WISH, YOU MAY INCLUDE SKETCHES AND/OR DRAWINGS.

- 2 -

IN ANY CASE, WE'D APPRECIATE YOUR TELLING US WHETHER
OR NOT YOU WILL PARTICIPATE. WE EXPECT THAT THE
STATEMENTS WE RECEIVE WILL NOT ONLY YIELD AN ENGAGING
(AND POSSIBLY HISTORIC) EDITORIAL FEATURE BUT WILL
ALSO EXERT A PROFOUND INFLUENCE UPON THE PLANNING OF
THE BICENTENNIAL CELEBRATION, ITSELF.

WITH GRATITUDE FOR YOUR CONSIDERATION OF THIS MATTER,
AND WITH ALL GOOD WISHES.

RESPECTFULLY,

*Leslie M. Pockell*
LESLIE M. POCKELL
ARTICLES EDITOR

The Expo experience was already behind me when this letter arrived from Avant-Garde. A bicentennial celebration is an excuse to spend a lot of money on things that are difficult to fund through any normal political process. What a waste it would have been to do an Expo 67 again or Osake 70 again, with all those little pavilions. The next one should obviously be a city. Obviously it's easier to propose real construction (hardware) than, say, new social programs. What if, to celebrate the bicentennial, free medical services were made available to every American, or housing became a guaranteed commodity, or a free and efficient public transit system was constructed to serve all cities on the northeastern seaboard?

But they were asking architects, so I decided to stick to my profession. I proposed an environmental TVA, circa 1976, with the hope that all three levels of government would spend money to create a new environment.

I asked myself "where?" Obviously in California. Why? Because a lot of people want to live there. It's a good climate, it's beautiful, it's growing.

This is part of what I sent Avant-Garde:

What to do for the Bicentennial, if not the obvious, a workable urban environment—and not to do it the obvious way. Two hundred years of nationhood have produced the wealthiest, most affluent society in the history of man without a single example of an urban environment worthy of its otherwise impressive capabilities. So, for Bicentennial, America will plan, design and build a 20th century city, will plant the seed for the environment to come. The beginning of a first new city to be followed by others across the country....

Bicentennial city will be an open city; open in the sense that its raison d'être will give man within it the greatest choice he has ever had. The choice to go and come as he pleases; the choice of what, where, and how he wants to work; the choice of recreation, pleasure, and culture; the choice of being in the busiest, most intense urban meeting place, or in the open country, still within his city, and alone; the choice of being with his tribe, with humanity, or withdrawing to the sea, to the mountains, to the forests. A city which is urban and non-urban, which is building and non-building; a city which is a region; a city where you are one of twenty million, and you are also one of thirty thousand, and you are one with your family, and you are one, alone—a city with hierarchy. The key to the city of choice is mobility. Complete and unobstructed mobility for man; so versatile and rapid, and impatient that you can be everywhere, in many places, not once a year or once a month, but daily, routinely. Bicentennial city would be generated by means of transportation that give us mobility.

We will be able in this city to move a distance of three or four hundred miles in a given hour. This will make our city three or four hundred miles long—a region city, the integration of industry and agriculture; or urbanity and wilderness; or hard and soft. Trains will move three and four hundred miles per hour, accelerating and decelerating as a pulse, faster and slower, never stopping. As they slow down to sixty miles per hour, local trains will accelerate and as they run side by side synchronize and coupled to each other in motion. Without waiting, man will transfer from one system to another, and again decelerate and transfer to another system and slow down yet to another system. Moving sidewalks and elevators, and inclined chair lifts in space, and trains, and subways; all integrated into a giant complex of geared wheels, all turning simultaneously at different speeds, never stopping.

In the 20th century, in an urban society, land and space are public commodities; therefore, they will be publicly owned. Stretching four hundred miles and many miles wide will be a tract of land owned by the people, where the people, individual or groups, lease, rent space and land for ten, fifty, or a hundred years.

Bicentennial city will be a federal city state. Any group of thirty thousand people anywhere within it will be able to incorporate as a collective. They will run their primary schools and their libraries and all kinds of recreational facilities and their internal policing and markets. They will receive a certain fixed

28. A plan diagram for California City.

percentage of the total tax base of the federal city to spend as they wish, providing their own community facilities. These collectives of various sizes will be federated into a city state. The City State will be responsible for the planning of the use of land and space; for planning and constructing whatever transportation and communication means which are necessary to give everyone the freedom of mobility. It will be responsible for maintaining the City State parks, the beaches, the mountains and the forests which will comprise at least fifty percent of all land in a regional city limits.

Thus, it will be the responsibility of your Federal City Government to ensure that what you breathe in does not poison you, to provide you with a free network of transportation which you pay for through your taxes just as today you pay for street cleaning, garbage removal, policing and the like. Undoubtedly, all this implies some basic changes in the system. For one thing, the proportion of gross national product devoted to the environment must, by necessity, be greater in a sophisticated urban system. For another, the proportion of the tax base available to the City State Government must by necessity be greater than what is available to the typical metropolitan city today.

Today people are rightly suspicious of big government spending. They have learned to distrust the products of bureaucracy, which are often ugly and insensitive to their needs. But consider the status quo. To say "I love Las Vegas, the highway strip, and Levittown" is a reactionary position. It means embracing the system that created the strip: the private exploitation of land at the community's expense, unchecked consumption, the settlement patterns and servicing systems that have caused pollution and destruction of nature.

We have to change our priorities in the spending of our individual and national wealth. I am always shocked by the way we spend money. Compare the fuss about the twenty million dollars it cost to build Habitat, or the endless debate about whether to grant each developer a third of a million dollars for the first phase of Operation Breakthrough, when the cost of one F-111 jet fighter is nine million dollars. A dozen jets are sent out on a sortie and four of them don't come back. Thirty-six million in one day, not to mention four people!

But if we want to stop pollution, sprawl, destruction of the land, then we, individually and collectively, must be willing to pay for it. There is no magic formula, no miracle technology, no wonder material, no automation, or any other trick to sidestep this fact.

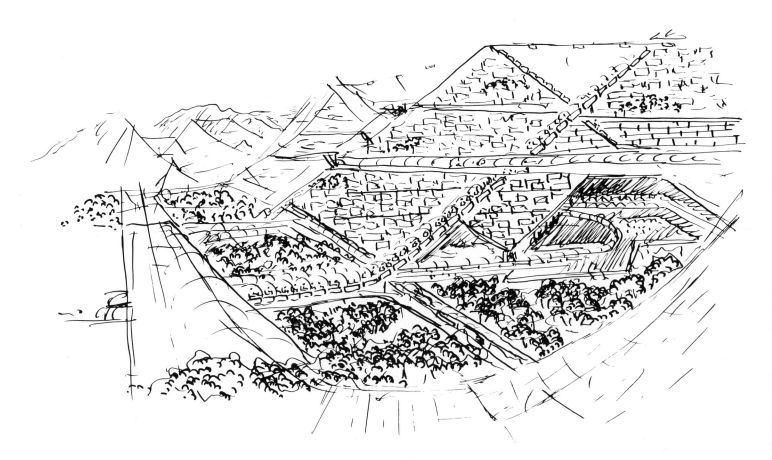

31. Housing membranes enclosing public and commercial spaces. Vertical and horizontal circulation totally integrated into the urban transit system.

32, 33. Diagrams for the Bicentennial City movement system, proposing transportation "loops" of various speeds. Moving sidewalks meet inclined elevator loops, which are synchronized to meet local subways. These link up in motion with express and interurban speed trains, forming a circulation network that is constantly in motion.

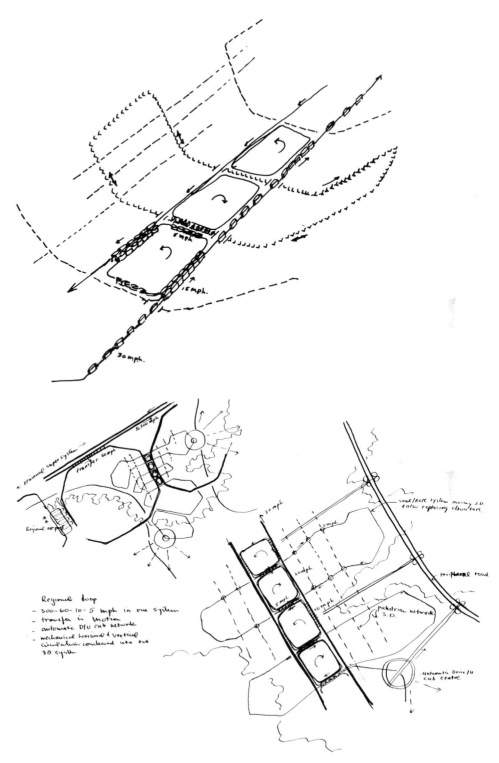

**Original Habitat Proposal**

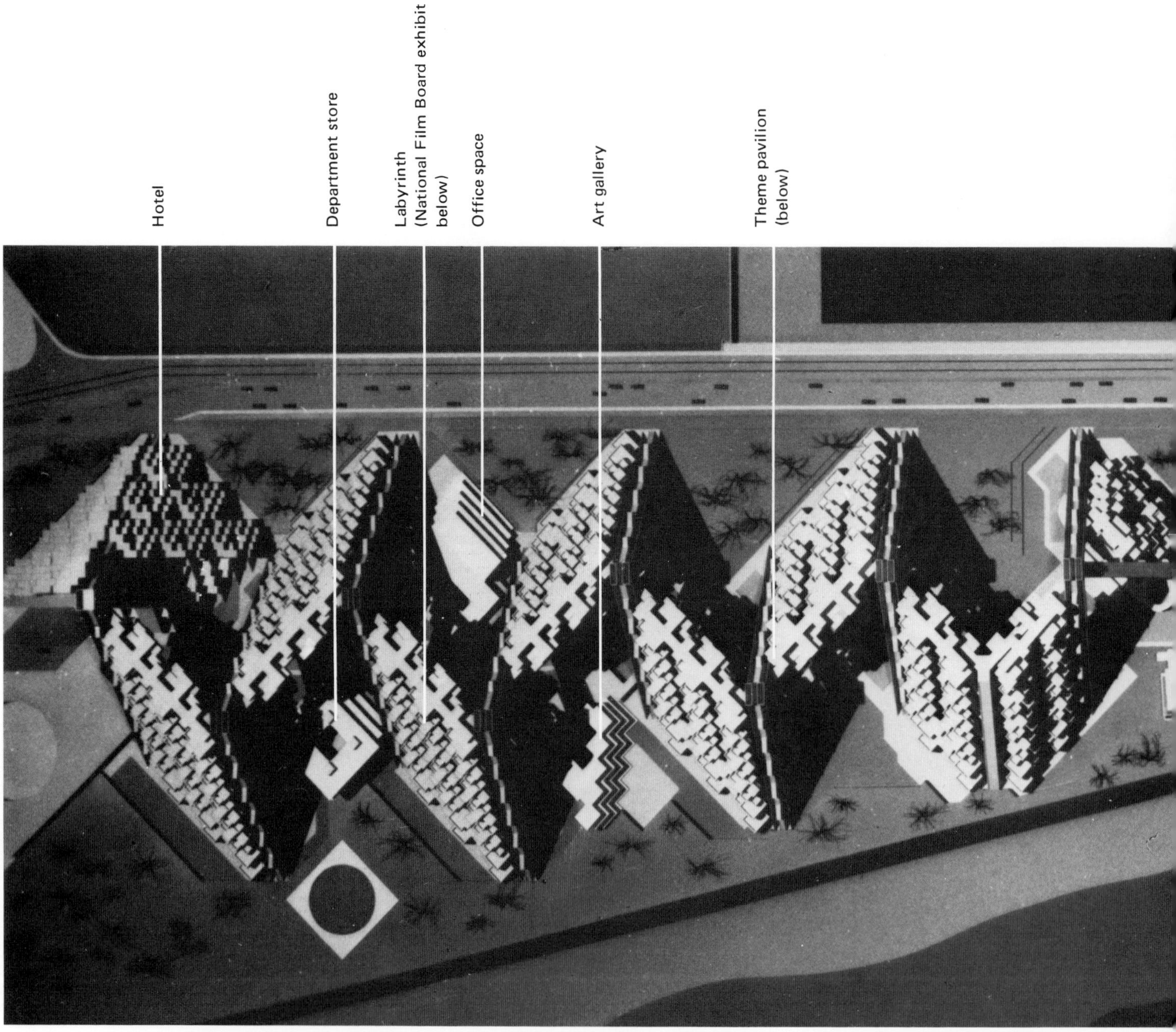
Hotel
Department store
Labyrinth (National Film Board exhibit below)
Office space
Art gallery
Theme pavilion (below)

34. Plan View of Original Habitat Model.

Service station

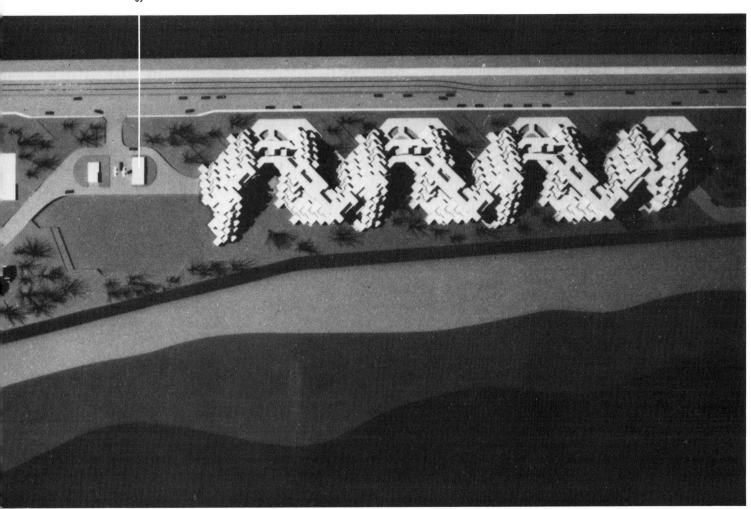

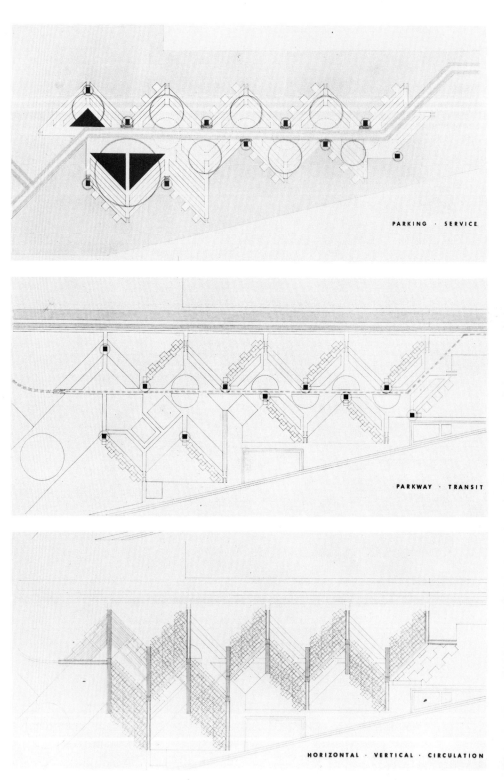

PARKING · SERVICE

PARKWAY · TRANSIT

HORIZONTAL · VERTICAL · CIRCULATION

35-39. Diagrams of land use and movement
in the Habitat complex on McKay Pier.

35. Relationship of roadway, car parking,
and elevator cores.

36. Public transportation and its relationship
to elevator cores.

37. Pedestrian streets and elevators serving
the housing.

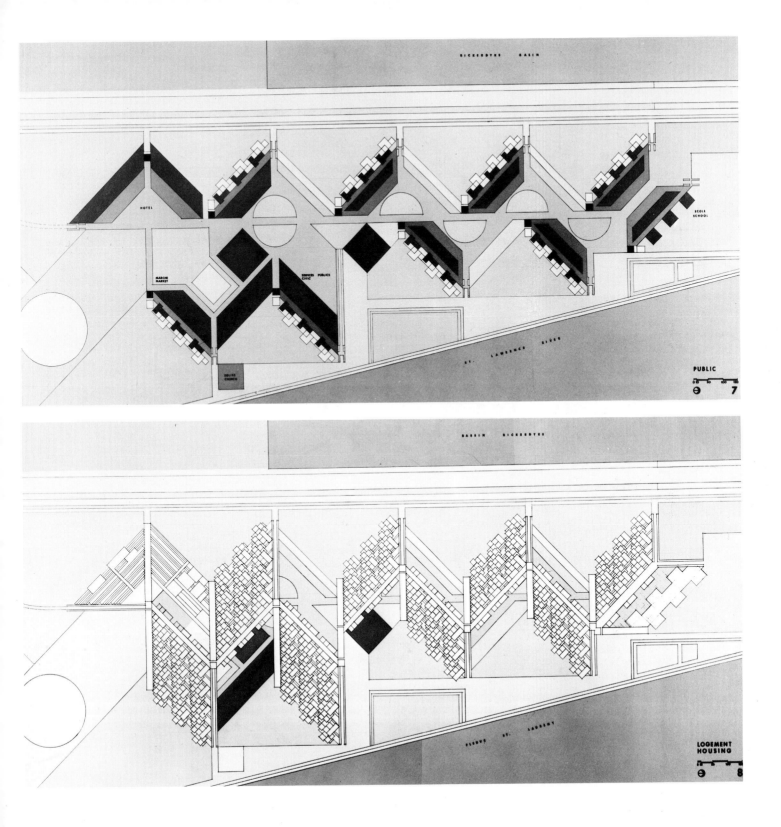

RICKERDYKE BASIN

HOTEL

ECOLE
SCHOOL

MARCHE
MARKET

SERVICES
CIVIC

ST. LAWRENCE RIVER

EGLISE
CHURCH

PUBLIC

7

BASSIN RICKERDYKE

FLEUVE ST. LAURENT

LOGEMENT
HOUSING

8

40. General view of the Habitat proposal.
Hotel in foreground.

41. Habitat 67 original scheme. View from
the north showing the public spaces.

42. Section through the hotel and A-frame sections showing the hotel structure and hotel superspace with its glazed enclosure, the ramp and parking arrangements, the transit system, and the department store all sheltered by the housing membranes.

43, 44. Habitat original scheme. General views of the original Habitat complex.

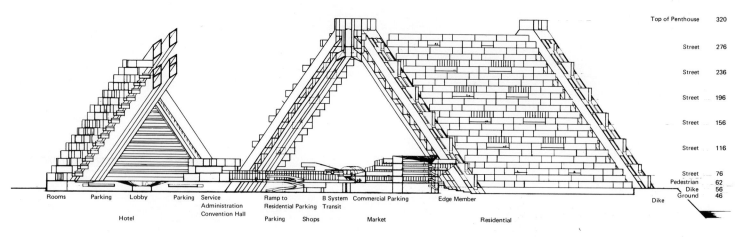

| | |
|---|---|
| Top of Penthouse | 320 |
| Street | 276 |
| Street | 236 |
| Street | 196 |
| Street | 156 |
| Street | 116 |
| Street | 76 |
| Pedestrian | 62 |
| Dike | 56 |
| Ground | 46 |

Rooms   Parking   Lobby   Parking   Service   Ramp to   B System   Commercial Parking   Edge Member   Dike

Administration   Residential Parking   Transit

Convention Hall

Hotel   Parking   Shops   Market   Residential

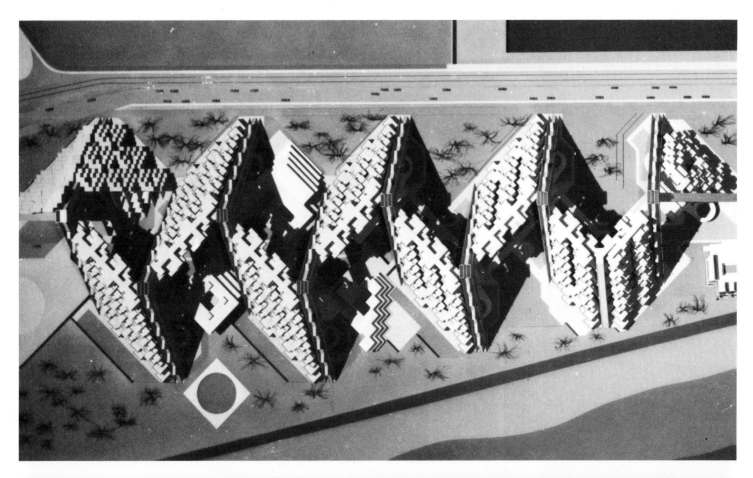

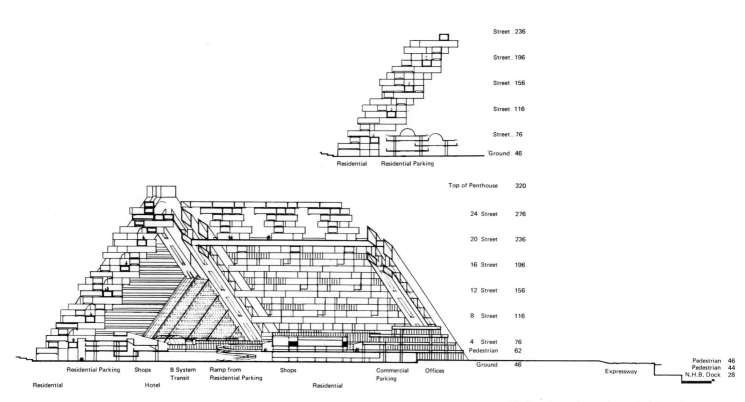

| | |
|---|---|
| Street | 236 |
| Street | 196 |
| Street | 156 |
| Street | 116 |
| Street | 76 |
| Ground | 46 |

Residential    Residential Parking

| | | |
|---|---|---|
| Top of Penthouse | | 320 |
| 24 | Street | 276 |
| 20 | Street | 236 |
| 16 | Street | 196 |
| 12 | Street | 156 |
| 8 | Street | 116 |
| 4 | Street | 76 |
| | Pedestrian | 62 |
| | Ground | 46 |

| | |
|---|---|
| Pedestrian | 46 |
| Pedestrian | 44 |
| N.H.B. Dock | 28 |

Residential Parking    Shops    B System    Ramp from    Shops    Commercial    Offices
Transit    Residential Parking    Parking

Residential    Hotel    Residential    Expressway

45. Sections through typical housing membrane indicating pedestrian streets, house units, and gardens on the lower levels; the parking and parking ramps are shown with the shops above them. In the background is the glazed structure enclosing the hotel lobby.

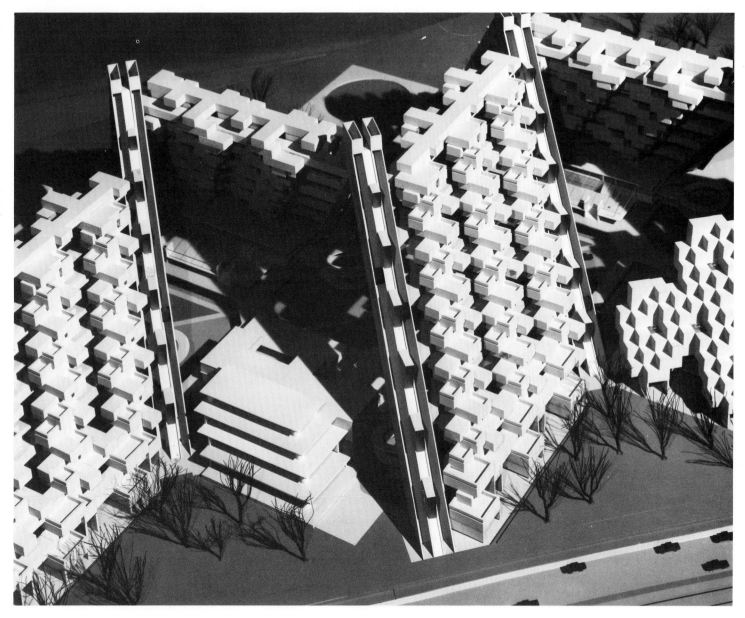

46. The housing stacked in a rhomboidal plane, consisting of twenty-two levels with a pedestrian street level penetrating through it every fourth floor. The pedestrian street structure is a box beam, within which the mechanical services and electrical services were distributed horizontally from the inclined A-frames at either end of the plane.

The modular units were load-bearing; all vertical forces are transmitted through the units to the ground, while the horizontal forces on the inclined membrane (such as wind) are taken up by the pedestrian street sections, which acted as horizontal beams spanning 300 feet from one inclined A-frame to another.

The streets act as braces against horizontal force but are, in fact, resting on the boxes for vertical support. The A-frames themselves are giant girders with the elevator tubes acting as compression flanges and the staircase acting as a tension flange. The two bottom legs of the A-frame are tied by tension cables underground in order to resolve the horizontal forces.

**Original Habitat Proposal
Studies for the Organization
of Public Spaces**

47-50. Alternative studies for the development of the public spaces of the original Habitat complex. Terraces of shops, office space, and exhibits are served by parking facilities below.

51. The scheme as it was finally drawn, with circular parking ramps, a split-level parking arrangement with shops and offices on the upper levels, a mass transit line running through the center and feeding horizontally to the inclined A-frames with elevators within them. There is a continuous zigzag pedestrian network that runs through the entire project indoors. In this original scheme, tenants could go from their house through the pedestrian street, inclined elevator, and through the public areas without having to go outdoors.

**52. Details of Habitat 67 public levels**
The Man and the Community exhibit was to
be located under a tent structure suspended
from the A-frames within the public area of
the Habitat complex.

53-55. Man and the Community Pavilion.

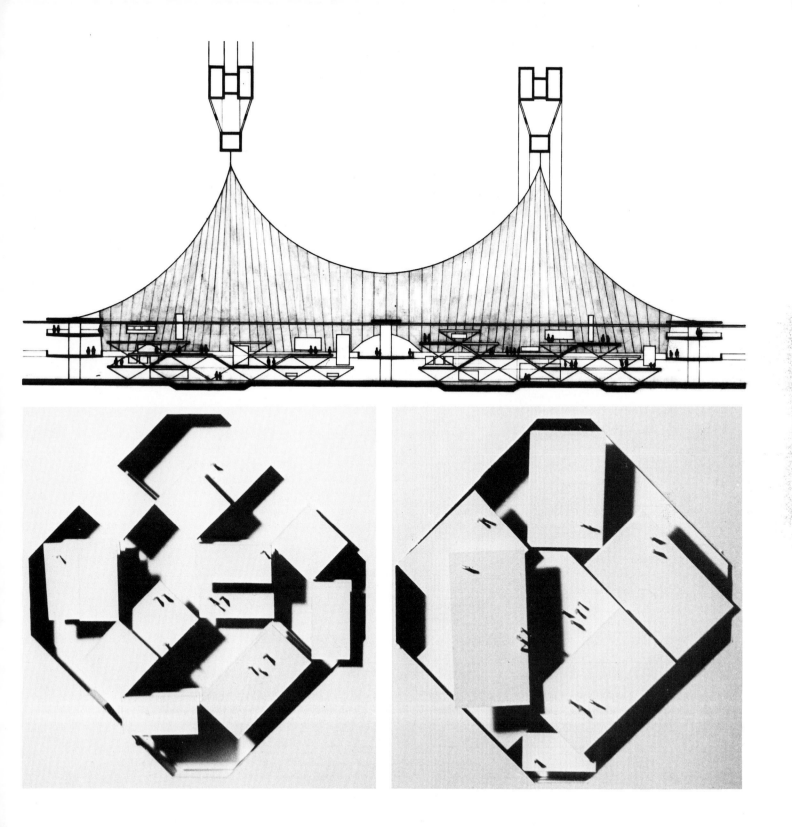

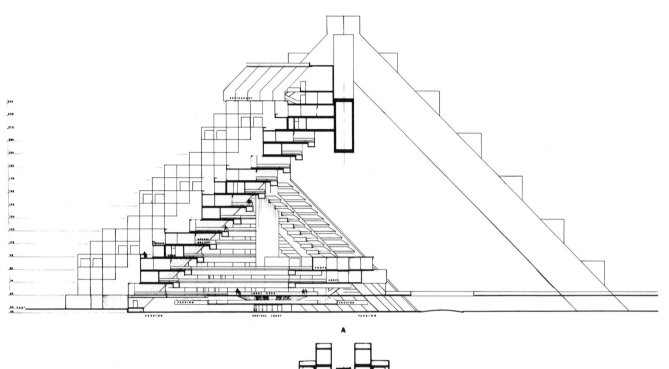

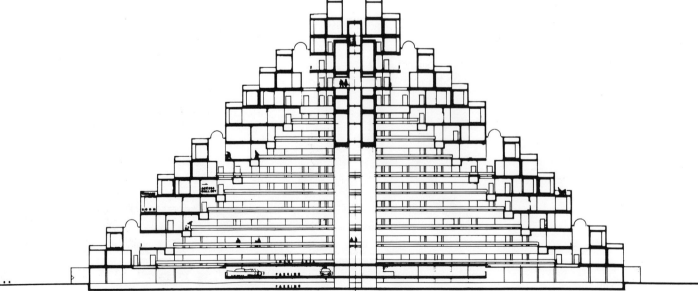

56, 57. Sections through the Habitat hotel.
A modified Habitat module, forming a typical hotel room, was to be manufactured in the factory. The units were stacked in an inclined structure with small terraces for each hotel room. The grouping of the rooms formed a large public space with access galleries looking into it. Convention facilities, shops, and other hotel functions were grouped in the glazed superspace.

58, 59. Photo of a model of the Habitat hotel showing the arrangement of prefabricated hotel-room modules and their terraces.

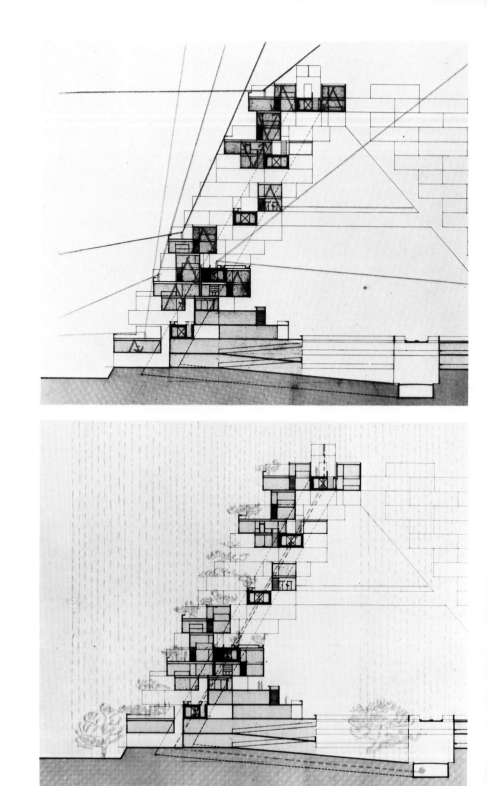

60. The section of the housing membrane is arranged to provide wide-angle views of the harbor and sky for each private terrace as well as light to the public spaces below.

61. Every house and terrace are open to the sun and the rain.

62. There were twenty-two house types
formed by combinations of one, two, or
three modular units of identical size. A typical plane was made up of three spiraling
groups of houses forming roof gardens as
they set back from the unit below. The typical rhomboidal plane was made up of three
columns formed by the spiraling arrangement of modular units.

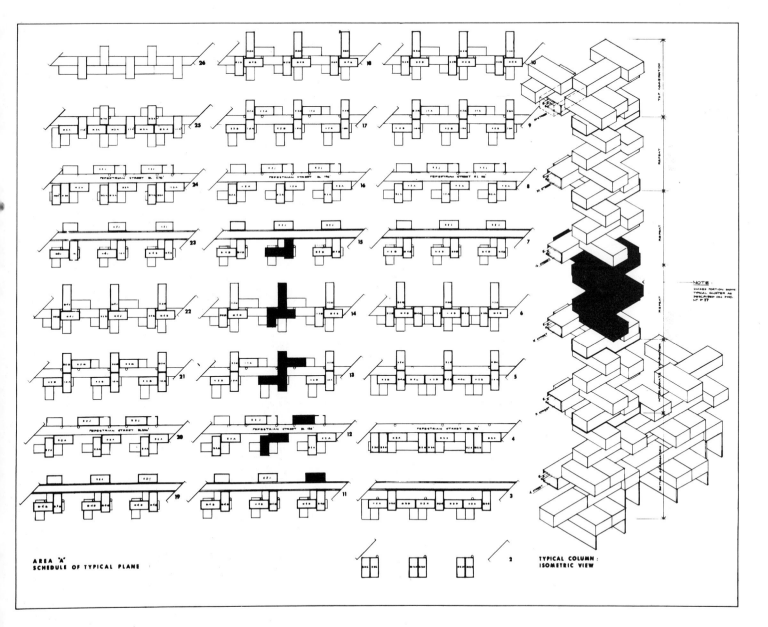

AREA "A"
SCHEDULE OF TYPICAL PLANE

TYPICAL COLUMN:
ISOMETRIC VIEW

What is the cost of "Habitating" (as a HUD official calls it)? Is it worth the price? Does it produce enough improvements in the quality of life? The issue has been raised in Fort Lincoln, in Puerto Rico, in Rochester, in Israel, in Baltimore, and has been the subject of much soul-searching on my part. Shortly after completion of the designs and feasibility studies for Israel Habitat, the administration of the Ministry of Housing changed. The new minister's emphasis was on maximum volume of construction and minimum costs, even at the expense of sustaining or reducing the prevailing standards. At the second phase of the development of Israel Habitat, private companies were brought in to submit proposals for volume housing. We invited the Canadian Polymer Corporation, which was venturing into industrialized building, to work in collaboration with the Clal Development Company of Israel. The minister, Mr. Zeev Sharef, in reviewing our plans, stated that he would like to know what it would cost to build the conventional three-story walk-up unit, with a central staircase (without projections or balconies), using a modular box system. He also wanted to know the additional cost of any improvements on this prevailing standard. In response to this, four designs were developed.

  The first one was an adaptation to modular construction of the conventional Israeli shikun, a three-story-high building raised on pilotis (columns supporting an open ground floor), with a central staircase serving six apartments; no balconies, no projections. The second was a similar arrangement of units but with the units projecting forward and backward to form roofless gardens for each house. The third was the loosening-up of the assembly of dwellings with the modules grouped in two directions, that is, perpendicular to one other; freeing the cluster, forming generous roof-garden spaces and a decentralized circulation system. The fourth one ambitiously combined the looser cluster with gardens and a pedestrian street system separated completely from sheltered parking and vehicular traffic at the lower level.

This gave a clear hierarchy of escalating environmental quality, employing the same basic construction system in each case. The cost projections were as follows: For the conventional design (based on an annual production of one thousand units and amortization of plant over five years), the cost was fifteen percent below the current construction prices. For Version 2, with terraces only, costs equal to prevailing construction prices (the additional cost of the terraces and the projection of the structure equaled the saving achieved through the volume of production proposed). For Version 3, looser cluster with decentralized access system, 10 percent higher than conventional design and construction costs. For Version 4, the "Habitat," with separated pedestrian and vehicular traffic, sheltered parking, on a sloped site, 25 percent greater costs than the conventional shikun structure.

So there is a cost to Habitating. Why is it worth it? It's fairly easy to say that in grouping people together to make up a community it seems desirable to make the scale of the family unit apparent. A steel and glass apartment building has no expression whatsoever of the number of people living in it. The opposite extreme is the casbah. The casbah corresponds with people's desire for identity and a notion of the scale of the community and their place within it. So the identity of the units that make up the community and the identity of each person's place are important. When you separate houses in space to express their identity, you create another quality of environment, one that is easy to appre-

ciate in Habitat 67. You live in a space that has views in three or four directions and gets light from four sides. It has open space immediately adjacent to it, so that the space expands outwards. The implications of this are enormous. The fact that you have a terrace outside makes a 1200-square-foot house in Habitat feel twice that size. The fact that you can go from indoors to outdoors makes the difference between feeling fairly self-sufficient in that environment or feeling locked into an apartment where you must leave the building just to get some fresh air. I could easily spend a whole day in Habitat without leaving home, because of the choice of being in or out of doors.

Another problem with most apartment dwellings is that there is very little that you could call "semipublic" space. I mean places for children to meet and play, for adults to stop and talk together. There are just those long corridors and then bang—you're on the public street. The Habitat "street" has many more possibilities. You have your "front step" and a walkway that has the dimensions and natural lighting of a real street. It has play areas and places to sit down and places for things to grow.

There are more complex factors that make a Habitat work. They have to do with scale, with our comprehension of the size of various elements in the environment, and with the richness and variety of spatial experience. They have to do with the difference between the feeling one gets in a plaza that has a hundred-story building sitting on it, with glass curtain walls coming to the ground, and in a square with three-story arcaded houses in a Mexican town.

It is easier to talk about building rationally in factories than about the enrichment of the human spirit through its environment, but both are essential ingredients in my work.

You could build a North African casbah—a four- to five-story and very complex environment using conventional construction—but not in North America or Europe, where workers receive high wages, and not at three times the density or height with the complex mixture of land uses that a modern city must have.

Very early on I saw that building identifiable dwelling units grouped in space and manufacturing them as factory-produced elements were interdependent concepts. Habitat could not have been built conventionally or even with a panel system. The panel system is too restricted in the way it carries loads, its connections, and its jointing. Space cells are both a method for building the kind of environment I want and, secondarily, a way of making possible a much greater degree of industrialization; the space cell makes it possible to do 80 percent of the work of building housing in the factory.

With Habitat we pioneered the use of space cells in large structures. Year by year, the lessons and failures of each project became part of the guidelines for the next solution. In my thesis (1960), I was still thinking about a vertical slab-type building, but with half of the enclosed volume removed, allowing light to penetrate through the buildings and reach the gardens. The next step was the original Habitat scheme (1963). Environmentally, two things happened. First, the vertical building became a kind of inclined membrane. The gardens are really open to the sky. The scheme proposed an integration of land uses, with public spaces within and underneath the structure. Then there was Habitat as it was built (1964-1967). After Expo, I branched out in two different directions: the New York project and the Puerto Rico project, one dealing with a far greater density than Habitat, the other confined by the budget of the FHA moderate-income housing program.

Building at greater densities in New York accentuated structural-economical problems. Putting boxes on top of one another for forty or fifty floors could not be done with the Habitat geometry. In our first attempt, we tried to take advantage of the rigidity and efficiency of an octahedral space frame. The problems were twofold. One was that the octahedral geometry was wasteful in space and inefficient when you tried to subdivide it for habitation. Another was that such a large and complex module created insurmountable erection problems.

When the site for the New York project was changed to Lower Manhattan, we

had an opportunity to rethink and decided to pursue a suspension structure made up of cables and compression masts from which the modules could be hung. The final form was very much governed by the rules of the suspension system.

In Puerto Rico we were limited to an FHA budget, and we had to conform to FHA minimum standards. The whole effort was directed to economy without sacrificing the environmental qualities of Habitat. One obvious direction was to cut down the number of extra precast pieces (streets, stair towers, and so on) that were not part of the box itself. I was looking for a shape for the basic module that would generate an external circulation system as well as an interior stair and a minimum of corridor space within the unit.

I first visited the point of Tropaco on Hull's Bay, St. Thomas, Virgin Islands, in 1969. I spent the whole day walking over every foot of that magnificent site with Bob and Jim Armour, the developers. Part of the site is jungle, tangled with vines and lush with vegetation. We broke through the tangle and were climbing on huge rocks that thrust straight up out of the sea, swept by the wind and supporting desert vegetation—clusters of small round cacti sprouting between the rocks.

I kept thinking that if the buildings could grow like the cacti on the site then maybe the land would not be totally destroyed by development. Maybe there was a way of building that was so much like natural growth that it would be more like planting large trees than "construction." It didn't disturb us to see trees on the site. And so I attempted to design buildings that would look as though they had always been there.

Later, I was commissioned to design a resort condominium, Indian Carry, in the forested hills on Lake Saranac in northern New York State. The client wanted "Swiss ski chalets." I could understand the qualities that he wanted, and I knew that they could be captured without actually constructing little chalets. So I worked out a geometry that lent itself to building with wood, with sloping roofs to shed the snow.

Tropaco and Indian Carry forced me to confront the issue of the "image" of a building, which for a long time I did not consider to be a critical ingredient of the design process. Rather than beginning with an overall "formal" composition, I was trying to design individual elements for a system that could be grouped in a variety of ways; so that the "image" would be inherent in the element itself and its connection to others—it would be the result of the system rather than imposed on it. In Puerto Rico we dealt with climate, for instance, through the way we designed the open spaces and the special shaded window, and the way we grouped the units for orientation and shade. In Israel the problem changed in magnitude. Within the same country, you have desert places that are hot all year round and coastal and mountain regions that have a fairly severe winter season. The image of the two Habitats in Puerto Rico and Israel is therefore very different.

It ought to be possible to achieve a dwelling unit for each family that would have everything that a house custom-designed for them would have. The walls and the windows and all the other subcomponents would be so interchangeable that there would be no need to have any two exactly alike. But of course, none of the projects that we've brought to realization comes close to that. There are many different unit types in each project, but it would be pretty difficult to rearrange their interiors. The relative lack of flexibility is something I have regretfully come to accept simply because I'm trying to build at $17 per square foot.

**"Proposal for a Three-Dimensional Modular
Building System," Thesis, McGill University,
1960-1961**

Three basic construction systems were proposed. One untilized non-load-bearing, factory-produced modular units placed within
a structural frame (System A). System B
placed those same modules in a load-bearing
arrangement. The third, System C, was based
on the use of prefabricated walls arranged in
a crisscross pattern. The proposal was not
intended for a specific site but meant to be
adaptable to a wide range of conditions.

10. General view of the thesis model,
System A.

**Habitation**
54-55
**Three-Dimensional
Modular System 1960
System A
Structure and Circulation**

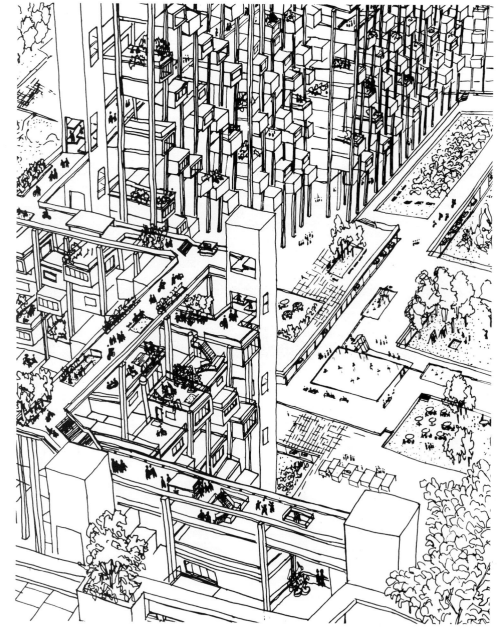

**System A**

The houses are arranged in a spiraling column with the mechanical shaft forming the
spiral core and the supporting structure at
the periphery. As the units step back in spiraling form, gardens are created for each
house as well as a stepping pedestrian street
running horizontally across the plane. Vertical cores with stairs, elevators, and services
are located at intervals. These serve one-way
up and one-way down and are linked by the
pedestrian street that steps toward the one
serving downwards. The spacing between
these vertical towers is proportional to the
height of the structure. That is, they are
closer to each other in the higher sections
(thirty stories high) and farther apart in the
lower sections (ten and fifteen stories high).
In this way a varying rhythm is created
which enhances a sense of location and identity within the project.

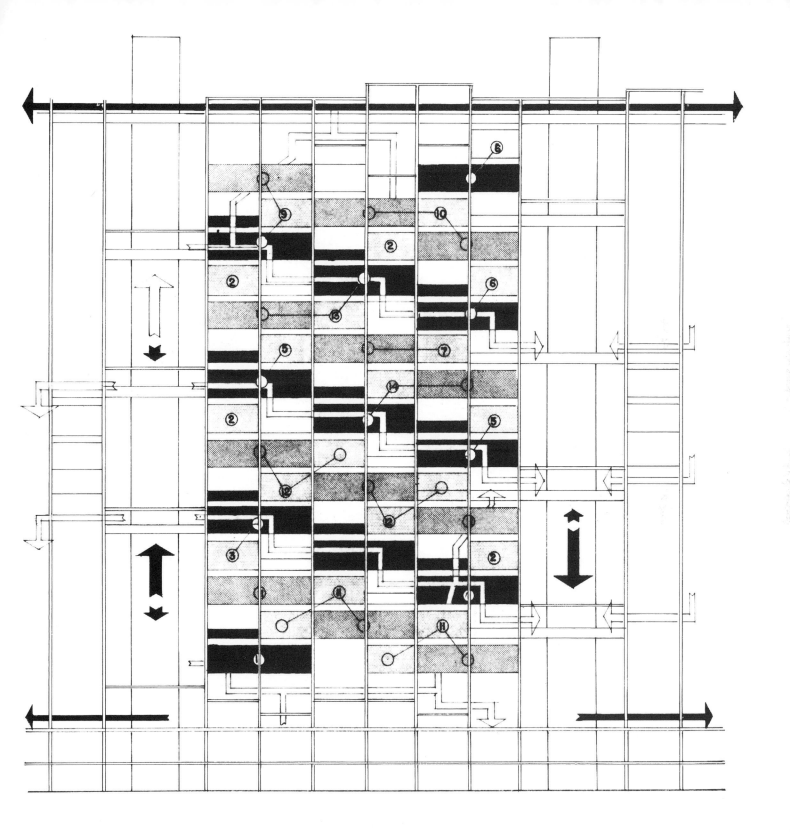

# Habitation
## 56-57
## Three-Dimensional
## Modular System 1960
## System and Dwelling Variety with
## a Single Repetitive Module

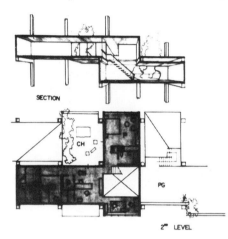

SECTION

CH

PG

2ᴺᴰ LEVEL

G

S

L

K

1ˢᵗ LEVEL

P

BP

PG

CH

L

KD

AREA INDOORS 1300 sq.ft
OUTDOOR PRIVATE A. 360 or 720 sq.ft
VOLUME 12,000 cu.ft.
NO. OF PERSONS 5 to 6

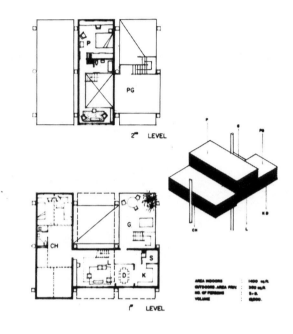

P

PG

2ᴺᴰ LEVEL

CH

G

S

D K

1ˢᵗ LEVEL

P G PG

CH L

KD

AREA INDOORS 1400 sq.ft
OUTDOOR AREA PRIV. 360 sq.ft
NO. OF PERSONS 5-6
VOLUME 13,000.

15. Detailed view of System A showing the modular units placed within the supporting frame.

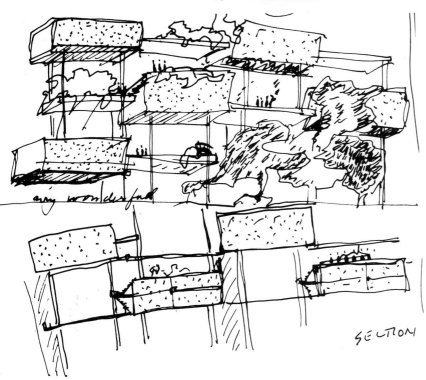

SECTION

# Habitation
58-59
**Three-Dimensional
Modular System 1960
System B
Bearing Wall Construction**

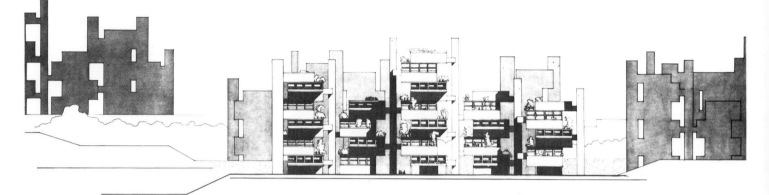

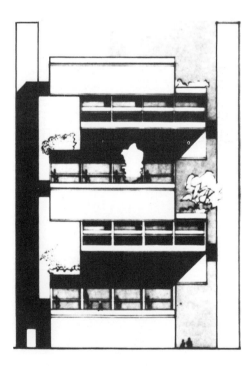

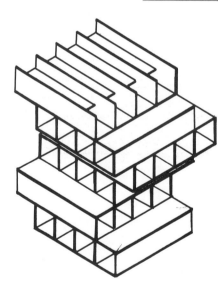

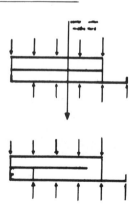

19. The structure is a series of superimposed walls perpendicular to each other. The walls and floors form an "egg crate" space frame. Wall thickness is reduced with height. Walls may be poured or assembled.

## System B

System B consisting of prefabricated wall sections assembled in a crisscross pattern was an attempt to respond to building conditions where limits on transportation would rule out the three-dimensional module.

The repetitive wall is designed to have sufficient structural versatility to step back in a crisscross pattern forming roof gardens for each dwelling—in a sense, an assembly of town houses in a spiral formation.

The clusters were grouped corner to corner with elevator towers serving two at a time and also permitting continuous horizontal movement every four levels.

22. Thesis, System B. General view of model.

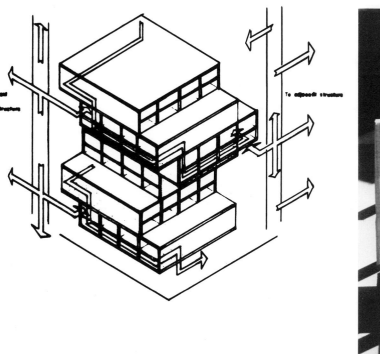

**Habitation**
60-61
**Three-Dimensional**
**Modular System 1960**
**System C**
**Load-Bearing Modules**

THE BASIC REPETITIVE GROUPING CAN BE COMBINED IN FIVE DIFFERENT WAYS RESULTING IN OVER FORTY ARRANGEMENTS OF SEVEN GROUPS EACH

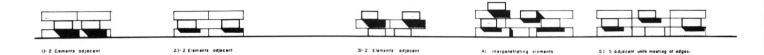

1) 2 Elements adjacent     2) 2 Elements adjacent     3) 2 Elements adjacent     4) Interpenetrating elements     5) 5 Adjacent units meeting at edges.

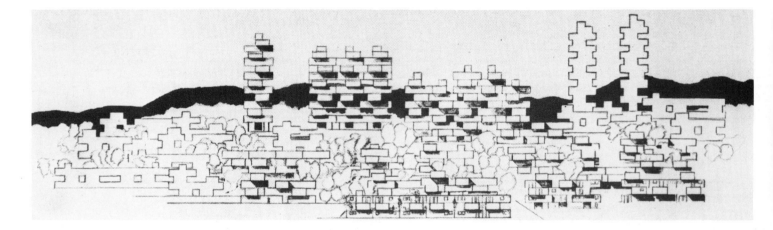

## System C

For lower densities, with structures ranging in height from two to twelve floors, the modular units were considered as load-bearing elements with sufficient reinforcing to take the load of the units above them.

25. Thesis, System C. General view of the system applied to a hill site.

## Habitat 67

Habitat 67 consists of 354 modular construction units making up 158 houses. The houses vary in size from a one-bedroom, 600-square-foot dwelling to a four-bedroom, 1800-square-foot house. In all, there are eighteen different house types, based on a single box whose exterior dimensions are 17 1/2 feet by 38 1/2 feet by 10 1/2 feet high. Covered parking is provided for all tenants, as well as additional visitors' parking.

Vertical circulation is by three elevator cores. The elevators stop every four floors, serving the horizontal pedestrian streets. Access to the houses is directly off these pedestrian streets, sometimes being one level above or below the walkway. The streets are continuous through the project, and there are play areas for children along them.

Habitat 67 is a three-dimensional space structure in which all the parts of the building participate as load-carrying members. The units are connected to each other by post-tensioning, using high-tension rods, cables, and welding, resulting in a continuous structure. Not only the units but the pedestrian streets and elevator cores carry loads; there are 28 post-tensioning cables in the longest street section; it might, in fact, be likened to a suspension structure.

All the houses are heated and cooled by a central plant; the street structure is a hollow box that carries all the mechanical services, including hot water for every unit and automatic irrigation pipes for all the gardens.

Within the unit, mechanical services run underneath a wooden floor; the bathrooms and kitchens are prefabricated packages. Every unit has an open garden and views in several directions.

26. General view of Habitat from the north showing the terraced gardens.

## Habitation
64-65
**Habitat 67**

27. General view of terraced units.

**Habitation**
66-67
**Habitat 67**

29. Plan of the plaza level.

30. Roof plan of the model.

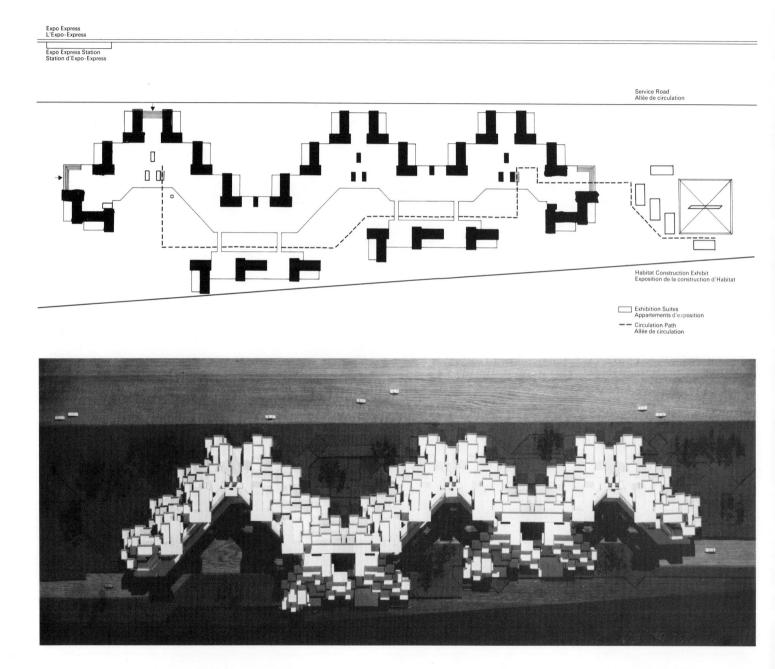

Expo Express
L'Expo-Express

Expo Express Station
Station d'Expo-Express

Service Road
Allée de circulation

Habitat Construction Exhibit
Exposition de la construction d'Habitat

Exhibition Suites
Appartements d'exposition

Circulation Path
Allée de circulation

**Habitation**
68-69
**Habitat 67**
**Street, Plaza,**
**and Gardens**

31. Section through structure showing modular house with gardens, pedestrian streets, and the mechanical and electrical distribution.

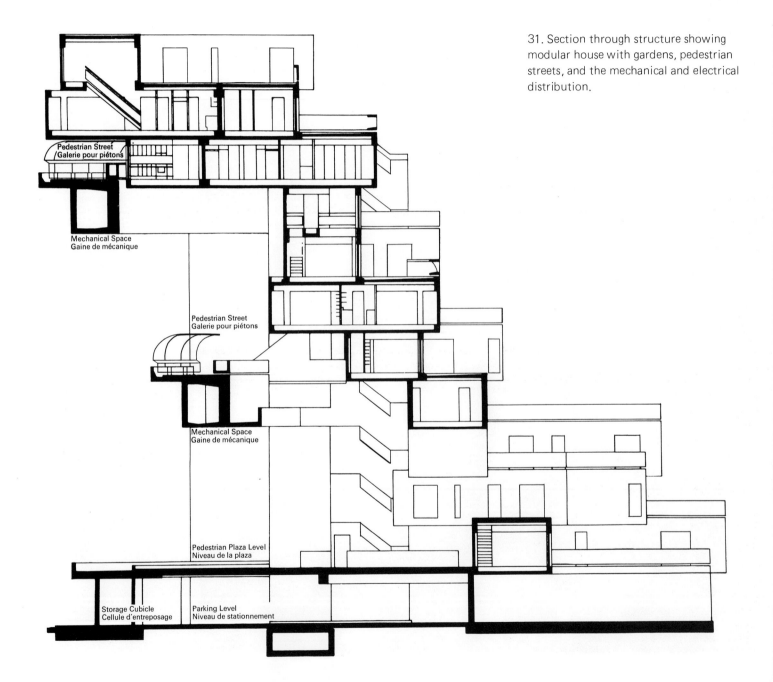

Pedestrian Street
Galerie pour piétons

Mechanical Space
Gaine de mécanique

Pedestrian Street
Galerie pour piétons

Mechanical Space
Gaine de mécanique

Pedestrian Plaza Level
Niveau de la plaza

Storage Cubicle
Cellule d'entreposage

Parking Level
Niveau de stationnement

33-36. The public areas of Habitat 67.

37. View of the pedestrian street.

38. Aerodynamic test model indicating ideal
shelter for the pedestrian street.

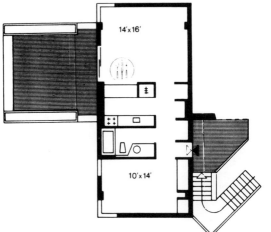

43. A two-bedroom house.

41. A one-bedroom unit with terrace.

42. A four-bedroom unit.

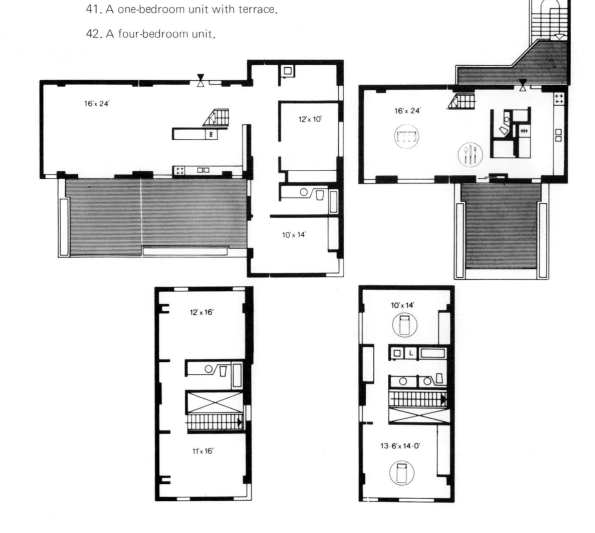

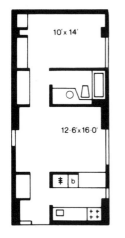

44. The simplest one-bedroom unit.

10'x 14'

12·6'x16·0'

45. A three- or four-bedroom penthouse with double-story living room and two large terraces. The living room is below the entry level.

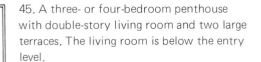

11·6'x16·0'

46. Exploded axonometric drawing showing the array of precast elements that were used to build Habitat 67. There were eighteen unit types in all.

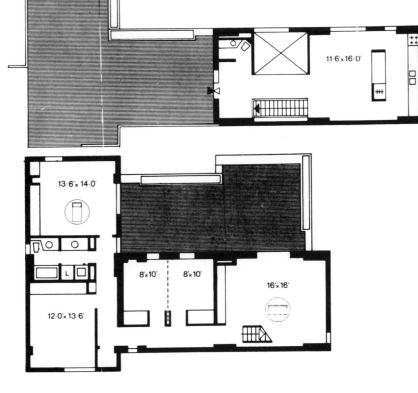

13·6'x 14·0'

12·0'x 13·6'

8'x10'     8'x10'

16'x 16'

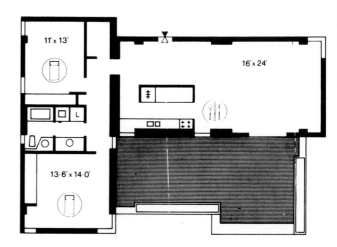

48. Two bedrooms on one floor.

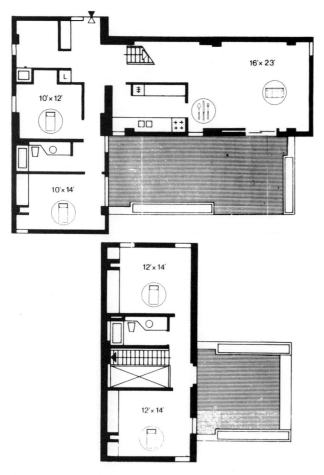

47. A variation of the four-bedroom house.

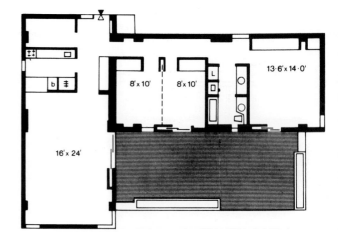

49. A two- or three-bedroom unit all on one floor.

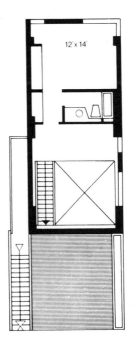

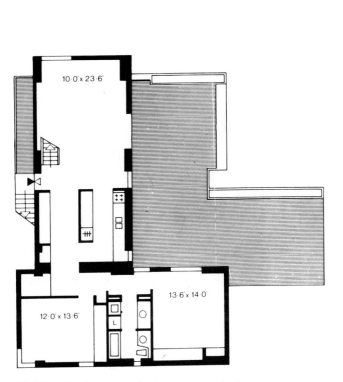

10·0' x 23·6'

13·6' x 14·0'

12·0' x 13·6'

50. Three bedrooms and a balcony overlooking the dining area.

12' x 14'

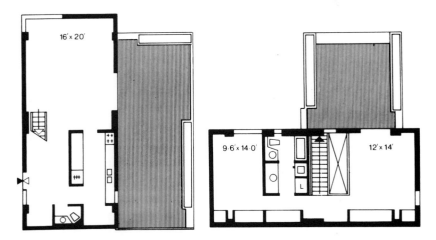

16' x 20'

9·6' x 14·0'

12' x 14'

51. Another variation of the two-bedroom
unit.

52-54. Habitat interiors.

55. The molded fiberglass bathroom.

56. The prefabricated kitchen.

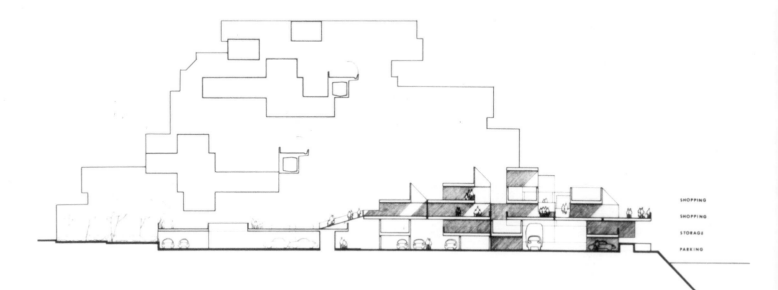

59-61. The Habitat shopping street: the proposal accommodated a regional shopping center totaling 300,000 square feet. Phase I of Habitat was considered as a first step in the total development of Cité du Havre and was planned to provide the first increment of shopping facilities for its future residents.

The shopping complex was located in the south cluster, to become a link with future Habitats. It was composed of modules identical to the housing module but with a modified roof structure, making it possible to construct it with the output of the Habitat factory.

The units were arranged to form single- and two-story shops with vehicular services below and a continuous pedestrian path linking the Habitat plaza with the riverfront and future development. The shopping structure was not realized, and cooling ponds were later located in the same place. After Expo, the building management opened for the tenants one convenience store in the garage.

62. Detailed view, Habitat 67. Aperture view
from the plaza level.

63. General view of Habitat from the south.

**Habitation**
86-87
**Habitat 67**

## New York Habitat I

This project was intended for a site on the East River of New York City, just north of Gracie Mansion. It was to include luxury housing, shopping facilities, a marina, and parking. Our intention was to construct it with modules of an octahedral geometry, with steel members cast into the edges of a lightweight concrete unit. This geometry is very efficient; Conrad engineers calculated that the steel members at the bottom would be only 8 1/2 inches thick, even though each module was 32 feet by 32 feet and might weigh 70 tons. However, the large modules, which were to be delivered by barge, created serious lifting problems for available cranes.

The structure formed an arch over the East River Drive, and included a shopping "bridge" linking it to the mainland. The shape of the module had structural advantages but posed planning difficulties. The apartments were large and luxurious, with two-story plans, skylights, dining bays, and gardens. But the smaller units used the space inefficiently and were therefore uneconomical.

67. Photomontage of the scheme on its site beside the FDR Drive on Manhattan's Upper East Side.

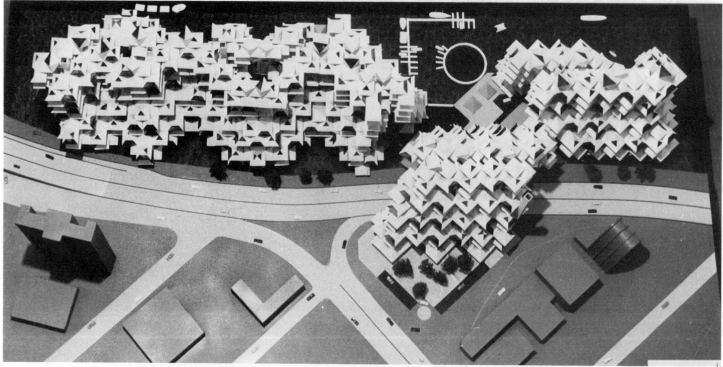

68. The view from the FDR Drive north-
bound showing the shopping bridge and an
existing municipal asphalt plant.

69. Plan view of the model.

70. Sketch for the basic structural geometry.

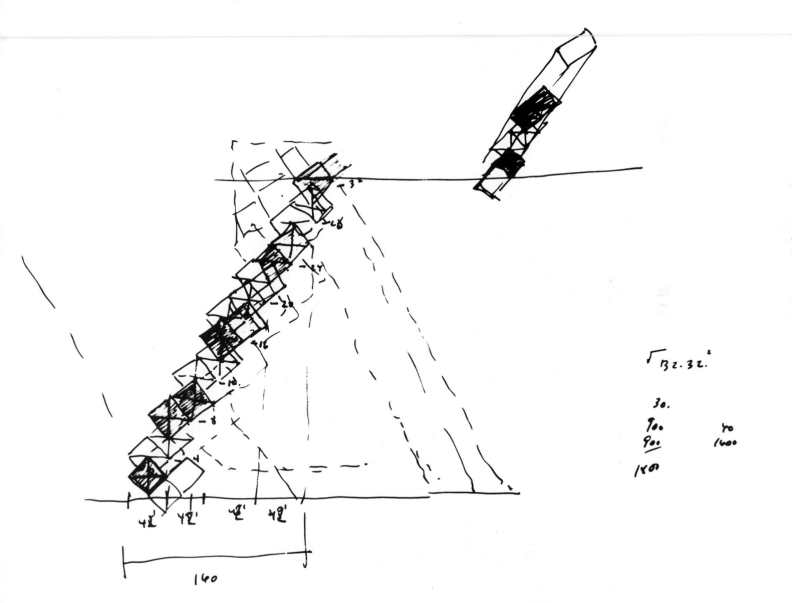

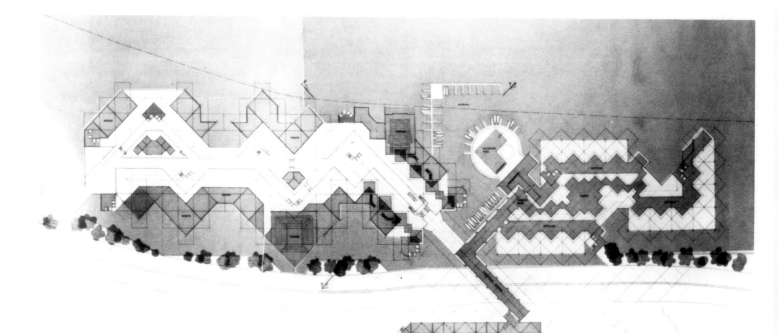

71. Plan of the main public level.

72. Section YY, showing the shopping gallery and parking.

73. Section showing bridge over FDR Drive and pedestrian and mechanical streets.

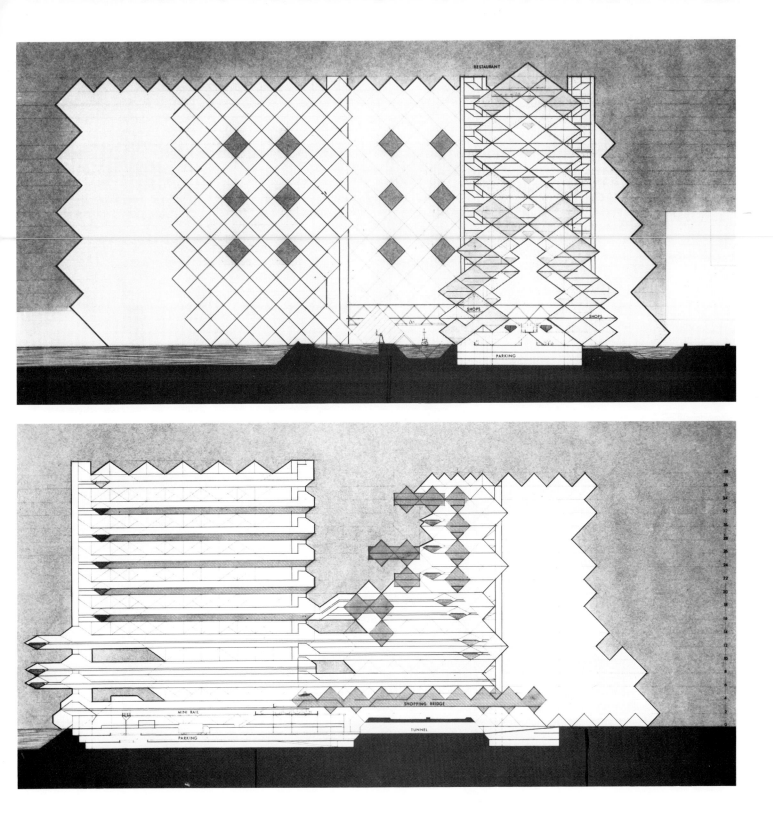

# Habitation
## 94-95
## New York Habitat I
## Grouping of Modules
## and Dwelling Plans

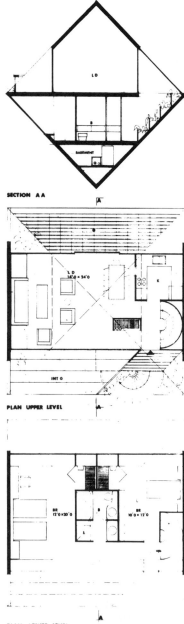

SECTION A A

PLAN UPPER LEVEL

PLAN LOWER LEVEL

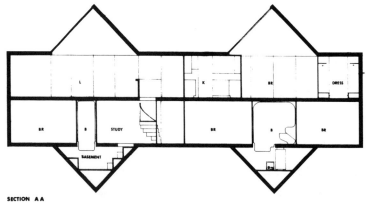

SECTION A A

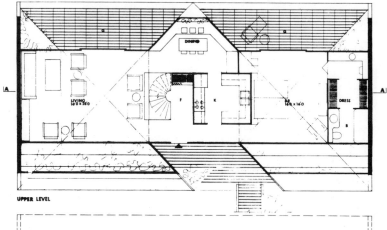

UPPER LEVEL

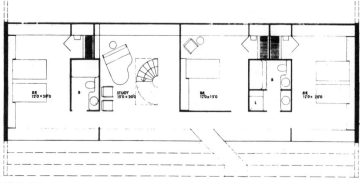

LOWER LEVEL

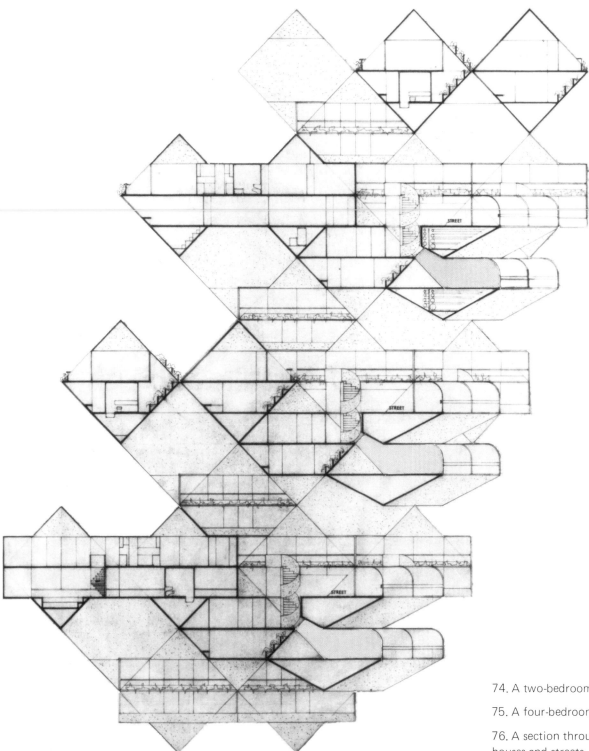

74. A two-bedroom house.

75. A four-bedroom house.

76. A section through the structure showing houses and streets.

**Habitation**
96-97
**New York Habitat I**
**The Octahedron as**
**a Building Element**

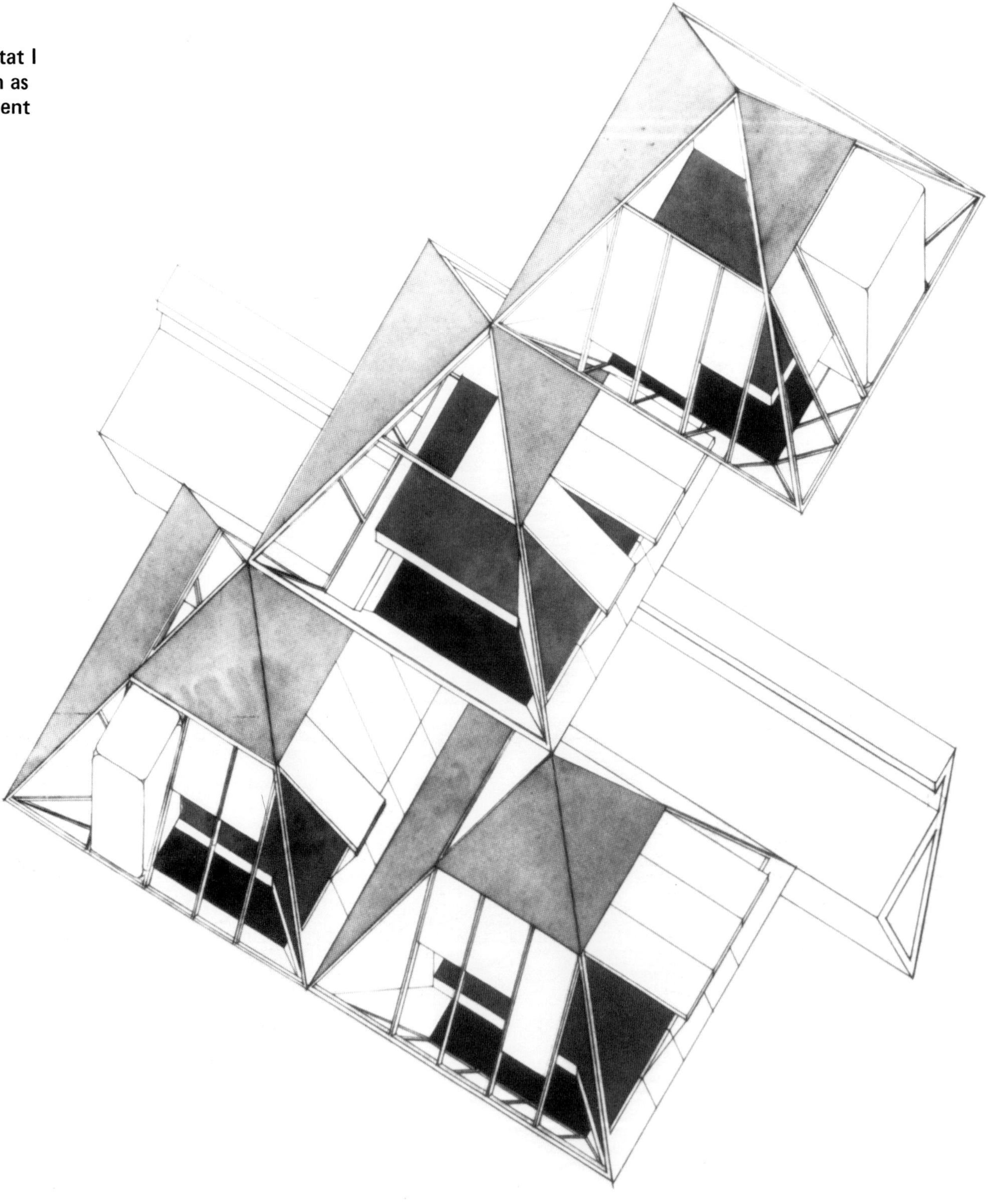

77. A modified application of the same geometry to the problem of housing in an area of lower standard of living. A module is constructed of a light metal frame with light-weight openable panels and utility plug-in components forming the dwelling.

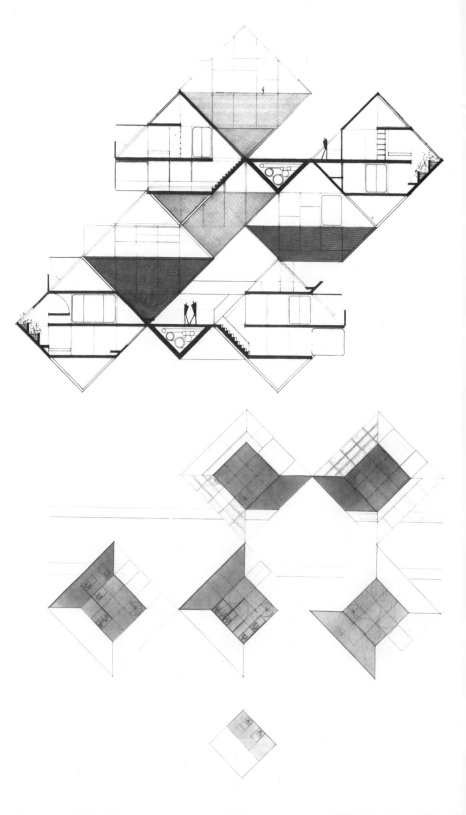

79. Section indicating grouping of the
modules and services.

80. Plan to achieve maximum utilization of
space for relatively large families. The dwelling is easily resubdividable at different times
of the day, forming sleeping cubicles at certain times and, through the use of pivoting
walls, opening up for daytime use.

81. A variation of the Giza module system in
which all service elements, including stairs,
plug in to the basic open cell.

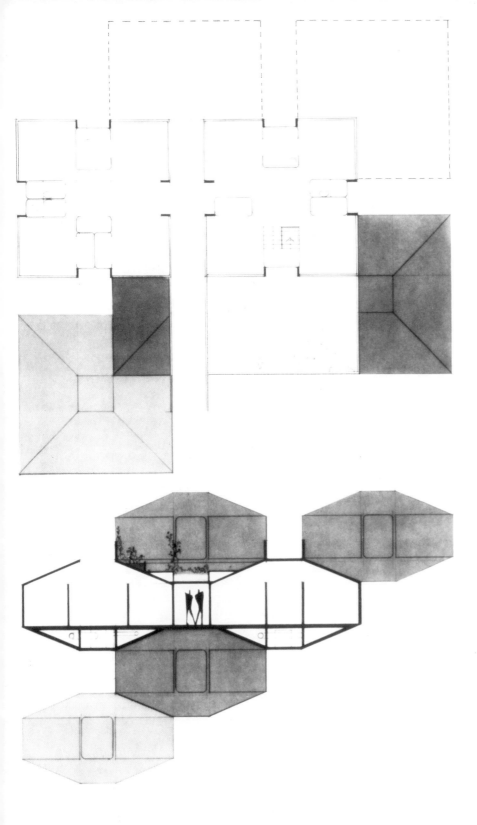

82. General view of New York Habitat II
from the river.

# Habitation
## 102-103
## New York Habitat II
## A Suspension Cable Structure

**New York Habitat II**

This scheme was designed for a site on the East River, south of the Brooklyn Bridge in lower Manhattan, with the proposed Stock Exchange to the south and a new ship museum to the north. The density requirements of 300 people per acre far surpassed previous projects. The city also required that the buildings should not form a wall between the city and the river.

With a light module it seemed possible that we could use a suspension structure that would act on much the same principle as the mast and the sail of a boat. Elevators and services in the mast, cables making up the fabric of the "sail." A rigid boom and a multileveled structure below would anchor the "boom" and keep it from swinging. The lower structure included 1 million square feet of offices and commercial space, including a hotel and a marina.

The modules, although they were stacked vertically, had both split-level and single-level plans and large gardens. Modules could be wide, since they could be shipped by barge instead of on the highway. The general configuration of the complex assured every unit good natural light as well as a magnificent view.

Both the structural design and construction procedures were worked out by Conrad Engineers and T. Y. Lin. The construction sequence called for the erection of the three service towers using slip-form techniques. Once the towers are erected, a traveling hoist is positioned on the top of each tower. The bottom compression boom is then cast on the ground connected to the tower by a hinge. The catenary cables are next connected from the tip of the boom to the top of the tower and tensioned until the boom rises to its final position. The cables are then encased in concrete and made rigid. The hoist then travels up and down the catenary cables, picking up the modules, which are brought into the appropriate position below.

Large openings in the boom permit the threading of the modules through it as they rise into position, with the highest boxes lifted into position first. As the modules are raised and the loading on the catenary increases, adjustments in the tensile forces keep the catenary constant. The vertical cables that hang from the catenary and are threaded through the modules could be continuous, running uninterrupted from catenary to the boom, or made up of segments extended with couplers as each unit is connected into place. The latter alternative is more convenient for erection but less efficient structurally. Once the units have been erected, the lower-level structures forming the shops, offices, hotel, and parking facilities are constructed and connected to the tip of the boom for horizontal restraint.

Constructing the parking facilities, which are partially underwater, poses another problem. One alternative is to build a cofferdam around the site, construct the parking levels and the superstructure, and then allow the water to return, using the weight of the superstructure to restrain the uplift force of the river. The cost of a cofferdam might be saved if one could construct three-dimensional modular sections that can be flooded and sunk into place. Once the superstructure is in place, with sufficient weight to restrain the river pressure, the water is pumped out of the parking levels.

84. View of the Brooklyn Bridge.

85. The slip-formed mast takes the place of a huge crane for lifting the modules into place.

86. A structure for offices and commercial space anchors the "sail" in place.

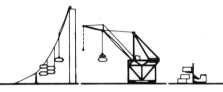

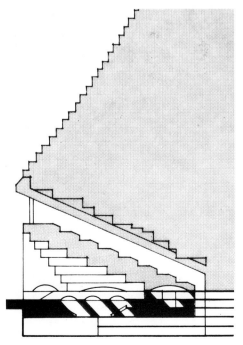

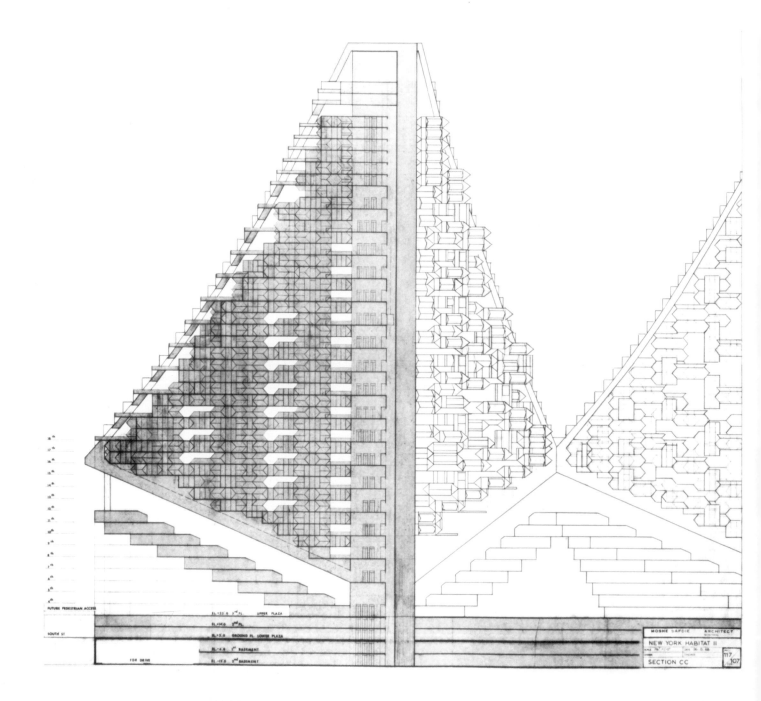

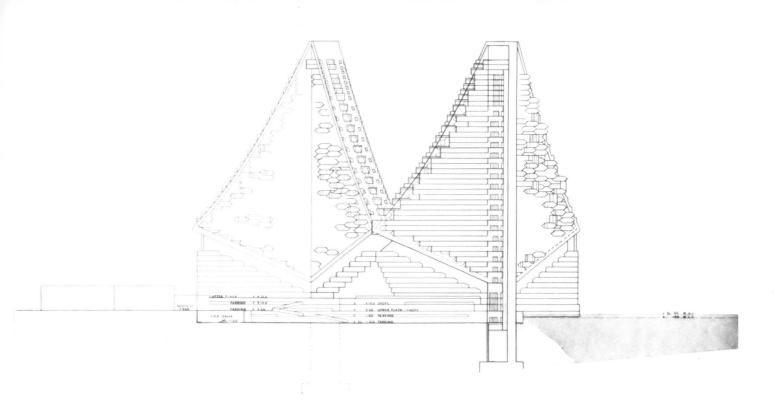

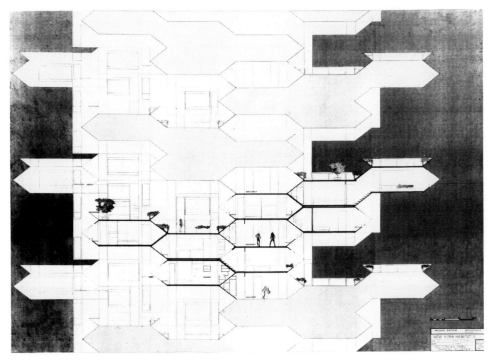

87. New York Habitat II. A section through
the structure.

88. Section showing parking, plaza, and
service towers.

89. A section through the "sail."

90. A plan view of the model.

92. A plan through one of the housing levels showing the enclosed pedestrian street system.

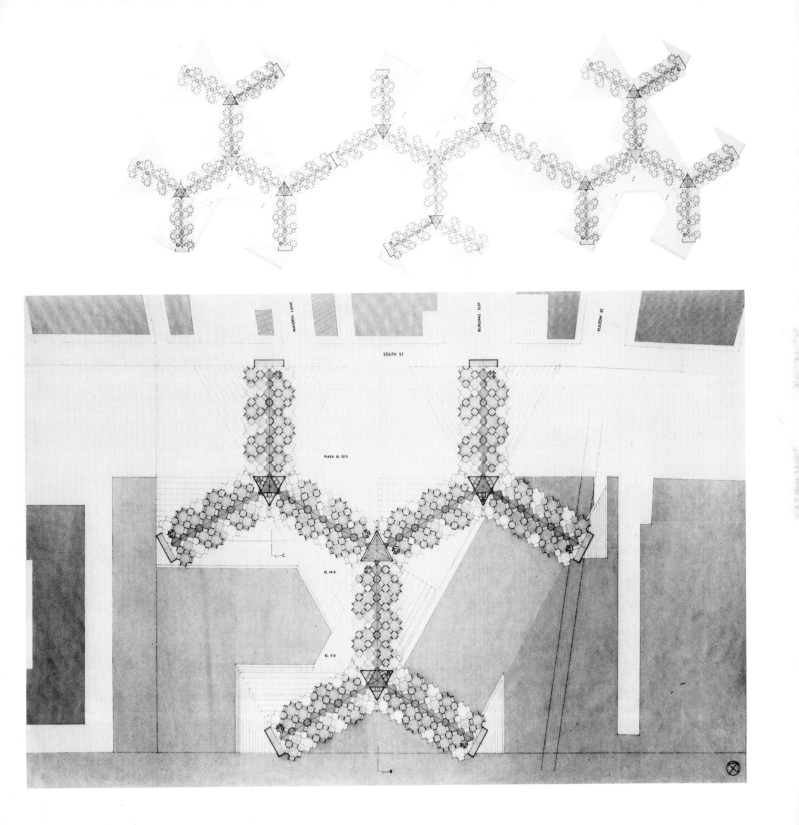

93-96. Plans of the repetitive four-story
housing cluster.

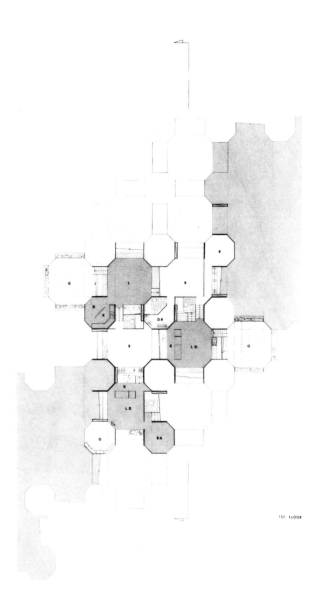

1ST FLOOR

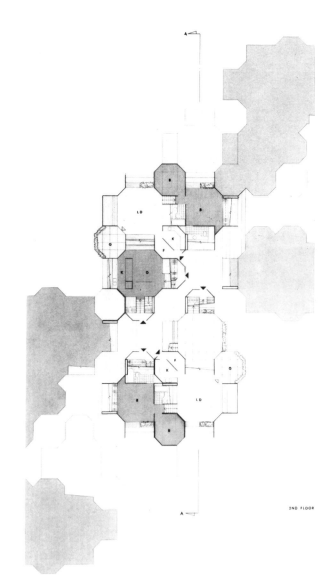

2ND FLOOR

93. First floor.

94. Second floor. Entry to half the units in
the group is from the covered passageway on
this level.

95. Third floor.

96. Fourth floor, another covered passageway for access to units. Some units have all
living spaces on one floor; others have a split-
level arrangement.

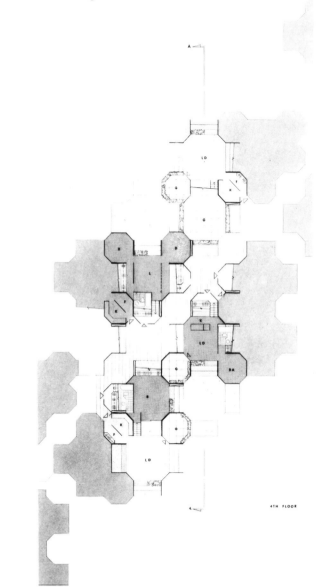

3RD FLOOR

4TH FLOOR

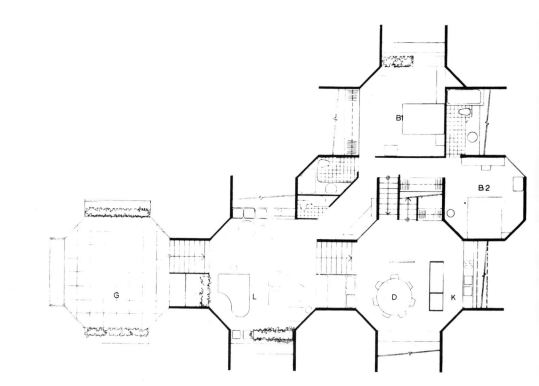

98, 99. Model of a typical unit.

**Puerto Rico Habitat**

The original Puerto Rico Habitat plan was
for an undeveloped hill 250 feet high, within
the San Juan metropolitan area and adjacent
to one of its major boulevards. Later the
site was changed, and the scope of the project much reduced. But from the beginning,
we were working within the limitations of
FHA-financed moderate-income (Title 236)
housing, and within a dimensional limitation
of a 12-foot wide module. In order to reduce
costs, we tried to find a single module that
would be able, by virtue of its shape, to provide the public walkway system as well as
internal circulation, grouped to form open
gardens with views, cross ventilation, and
sheltered parking. We were trying to elimi-
nate all the extra precast components (access stairs, street sections, and so forth) that
Habitat 67 had required.

   The facts that we were building on a hill
and that the structure was never more than
six stories helped to simplify the overall system. The basic cluster had not only to provide proper access to every unit, a terrace,
privacy, and view but also vertical and horizontal circulation through the site. Pedestrian movement is always kept separate from
vehicular traffic. We achieved much greater
economy, but the greater complexity of the
design process is reflected in the fact that
the Habitat 67 cluster took us two months
in the office, while the Puerto Rico project
took eight months. We talked to engineers
about the possibility of using a computer to
keep track of the variables. They told us it
would take five years to write the program.

The module is cast in concrete, with 3 1/2-inch walls and 4-inch slabs. Each box is 430 square feet in area and weighs approximately 22 tons. (The basic box for Habitat 67 weighed 70 tons.) The split-level plan allows up to three boxes to be joined to form one unit, with a minimum amount of internal circulation area.

101. The original Hato Rey site and its environs.

**Habitation**
116-117
**Puerto Rico Habitat**
**Proposal for the Original Site**

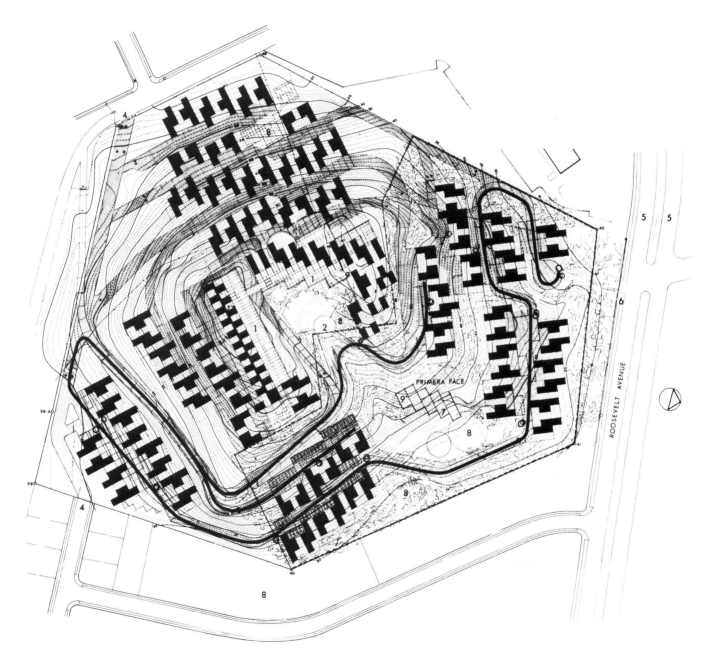

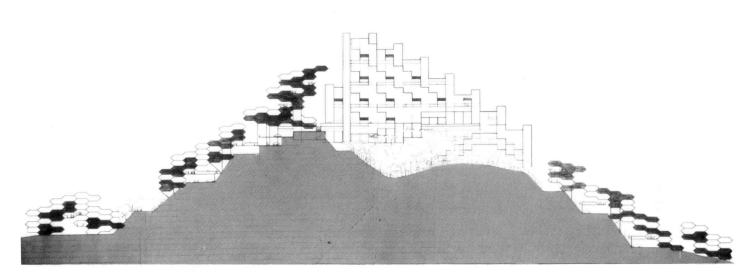

103. Plan of the original Hato Rey Puerto
Rico Habitat site accommodating 800 housing units, community and commercial center, and generous public park space to the
gross average density of 40 units to the acre.

104. A section through the site.

pattern of development
on hill itself
has much flexibility

105. Early sketches for Puerto Rico Habitat.

106. Plan view of the site model.

107. Site plan for the second site located in the Berwin Farm area of San Juan.

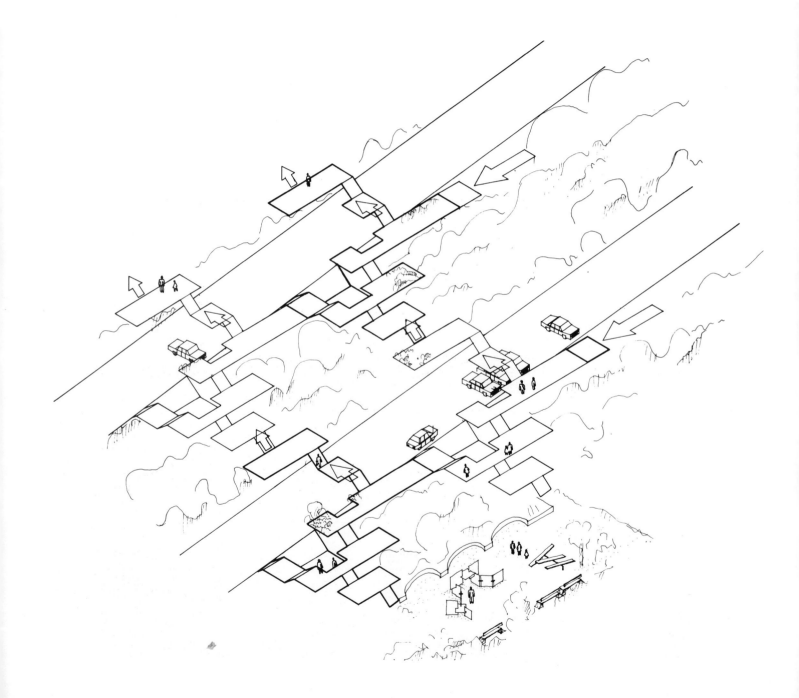

108. Diagram showing the relationship of
vehicular and pedestrian movement on the
site.

109. Section through the hillside housing indicating access system generated by shape of
the module (also covered parking).

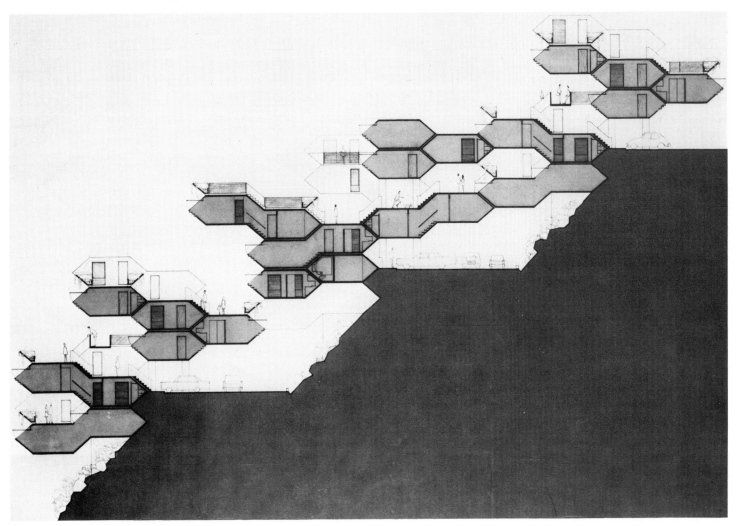

**Habitation**
122-123
**Puerto Rico Habitat**
**Typical Module and**
**Permutations**

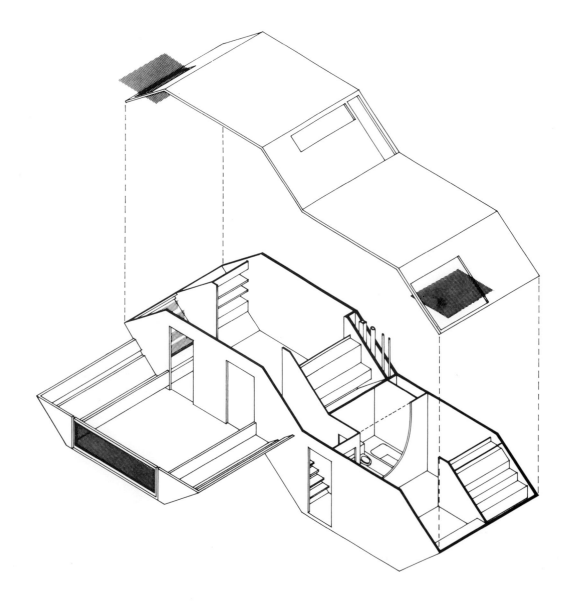

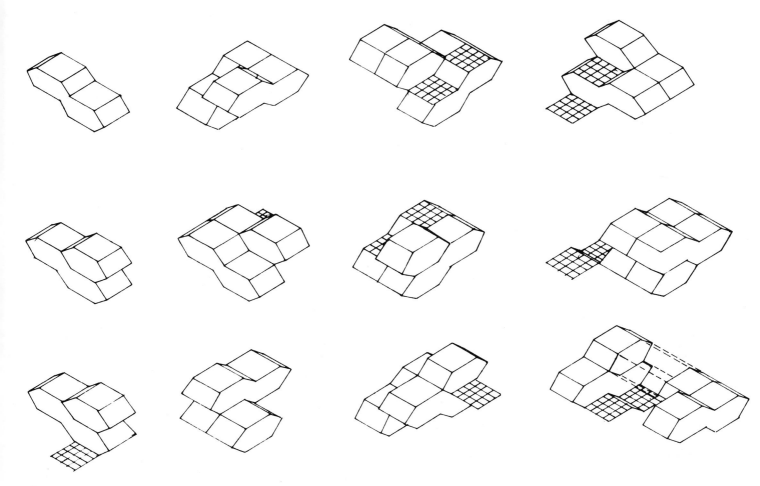

110. Exploded isometric view of the Puerto Rico module with details for planters, kitchens and baths, storage, the shaded window, and stairs.

111. Various unit types.

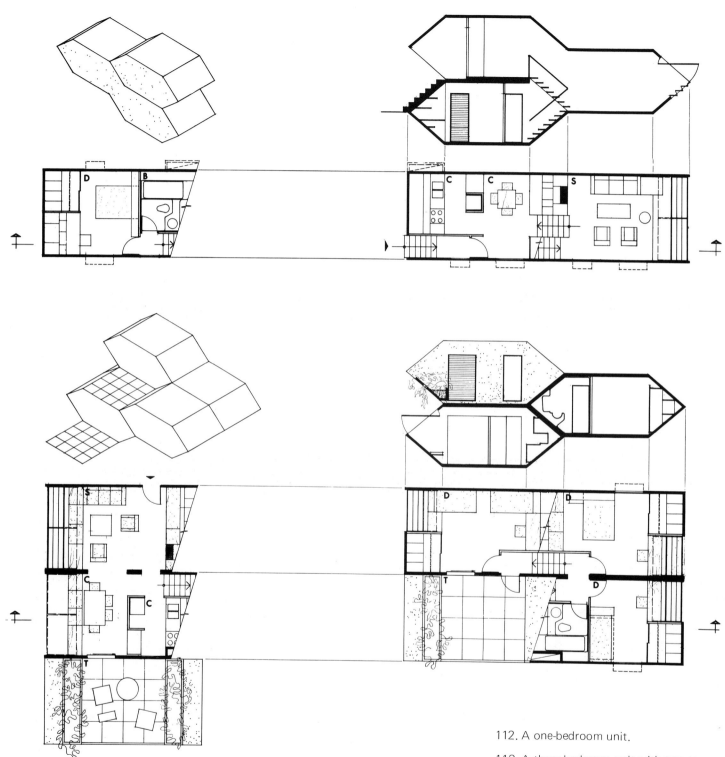

112. A one-bedroom unit.

113. A three-bedroom unit with two terraces.

115. The view from the walkway system.

116. The cantilevered structure forms sheltered parking areas below. Pedestrian and vehicular paths never cross at the same level.

119. Park space and amphitheater at the crest of the hill (on the Hato Rey site).

120. Exploded isometric showing the components of the system.

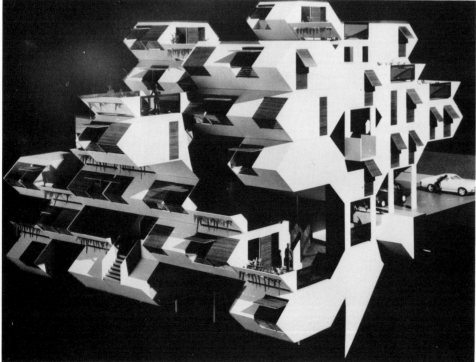

**Habitation**
130-131
**Low-Density Housing
for Puerto Rico**

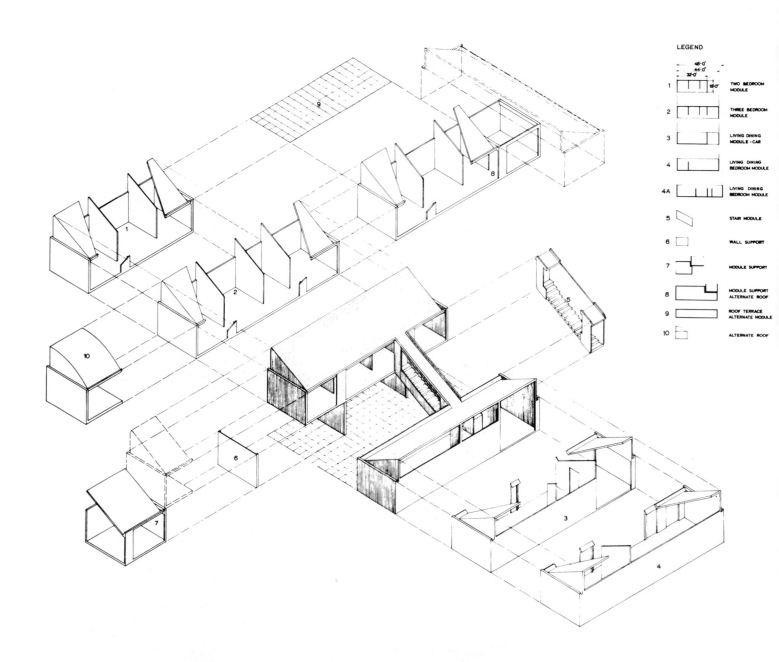

LEGEND

| | | |
|---|---|---|
| 1 | | TWO BEDROOM MODULE |
| 2 | | THREE BEDROOM MODULE |
| 3 | | LIVING DINING MODULE - CAR |
| 4 | | LIVING DINING BEDROOM MODULE |
| 4A | | LIVING DINING BEDROOM MODULE |
| 5 | | STAIR MODULE |
| 6 | | WALL SUPPORT |
| 7 | | MODULE SUPPORT |
| 8 | | MODULE SUPPORT ALTERNATE ROOF |
| 9 | | ROOF TERRACE ALTERNATE MODULE |
| 10 | | ALTERNATE ROOF |

## Low-Density Housing System, Puerto Rico

We were commissioned to consider utilizing the Puerto Rico Habitat factory output for a housing system that could be used on conventional lots, that is, 40, 50, and 60 feet wide, as well as for slightly higher density maisonnettes and town houses. The modules are to be produced at an off-site factory, and therefore again limited to 12 feet width. The basic arrangement is made up of two boxes, one with the major living spaces placed on grade, the other raised one story and connected to the living space by an additional stairway element. This forms a patio house with some sheltered outdoor area and considerable privacy for each unit. Site work—roads, foundations, and even landscaping—would be completed before the units are placed into position.

The juxtaposition of the two units with patio space between them gives a feeling of spaciousness, even though the building area is minimal (800 to 1100 square feet), and the blank walls of adjacent houses are used to give privacy to the outdoor spaces, expanding the effective living space of the family.

121. Aerial view of single-family houses in San Juan, Puerto Rico.

**Habitation**
132-133
**Low-Density Housing
for Puerto Rico
Adapting to an Existing
Subdivision**

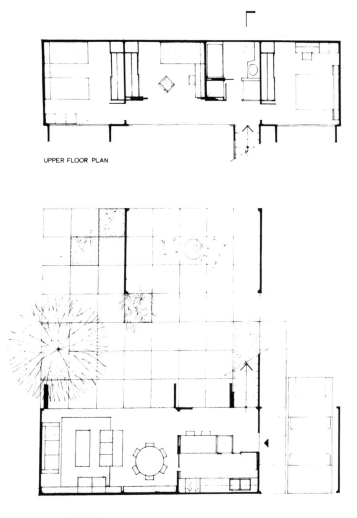

UPPER FLOOR PLAN

LOWER FLOOR PLAN

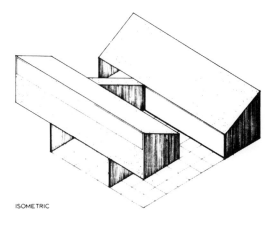

ISOMETRIC

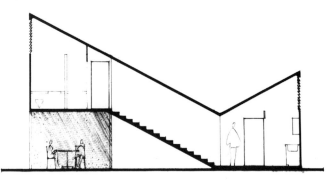

SECTION

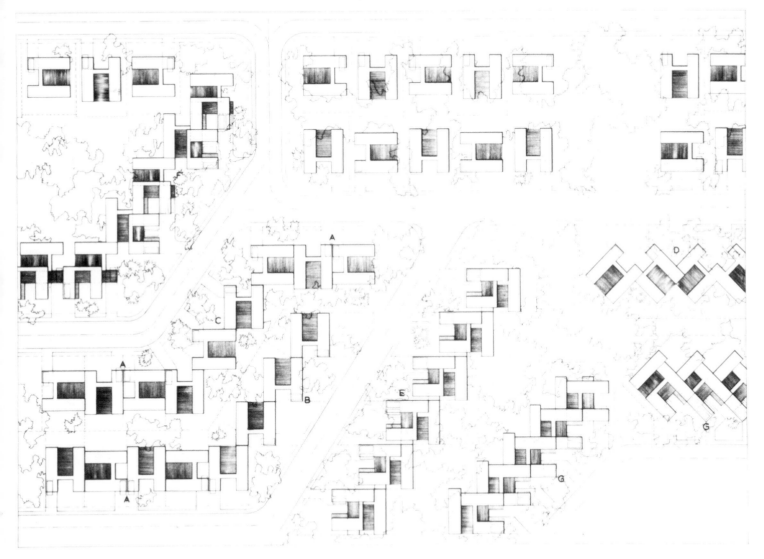

124. A subdivision plan showing various
ways that the units can be joined and
adapted to an existing subdivision.

Habitation
134-135
Low-Density Housing
for Puerto Rico
Improving on Suburban
Densities

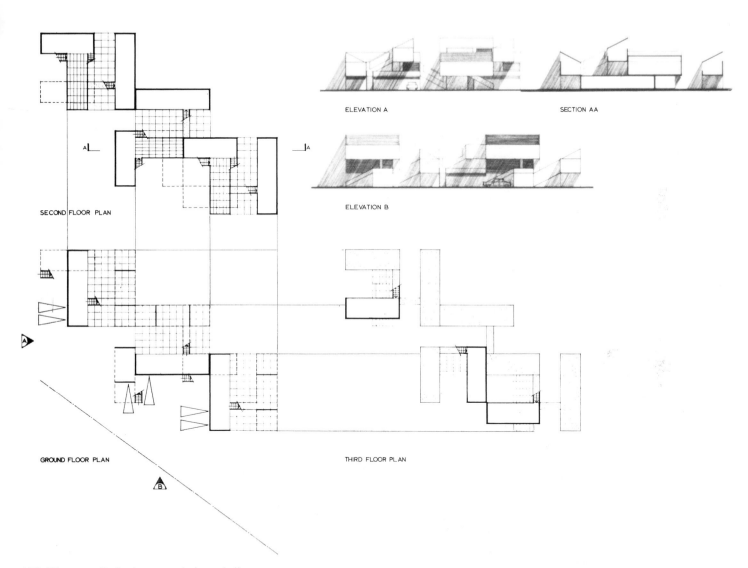

SECOND FLOOR PLAN

GROUND FLOOR PLAN

A

B

ELEVATION A

SECTION AA

ELEVATION B

THIRD FLOOR PLAN

126. When not limited to an existing subdivision, a more versatile grouping of the units is possible, increasing the density to 12 units per acre and increasing the privacy and efficiency of the private and public outdoor spaces.

**Tropaco Resort Condominium,
Hull's Bay, St. Thomas,
U.S. Virgin Islands**

The site for this development is a spectacular rocky peninsula on the island of St. Thomas. There were to be 180 units, both of the hotel type and condominium home type; many homeowners were expected to rent out their units to groups of vacationers for at least part of the year, so it was desirable to be able to convert homes into several hotel rooms with a shared lounge. The modular elements were to be shipped by barge from a factory in Puerto Rico.

Our objective was to disturb the natural site and its plant life as little as possible. In response to this, the system evolved into two basic components. An octagonally shaped cylindrical element that was stacked vertically acts as a support column for the structure, accommodates bathrooms, kitchens, and other items requiring wet services, with the bottom cylinder acting as a water cistern for the water collected on the roofs. The columns thus formed minimized the number of foundation points and the cutting and filling required on the site.

The living units of a more complex geometry were attached to the cylindrical columns that formed greater clusters supported by four cylinders at a time. The living units were designed for convertible living, opening up with overhanging shaded shutters, when air conditioning was desired.

127. Hull's Bay, St. Thomas, U.S. Virgin Islands.

128. Photomontage.

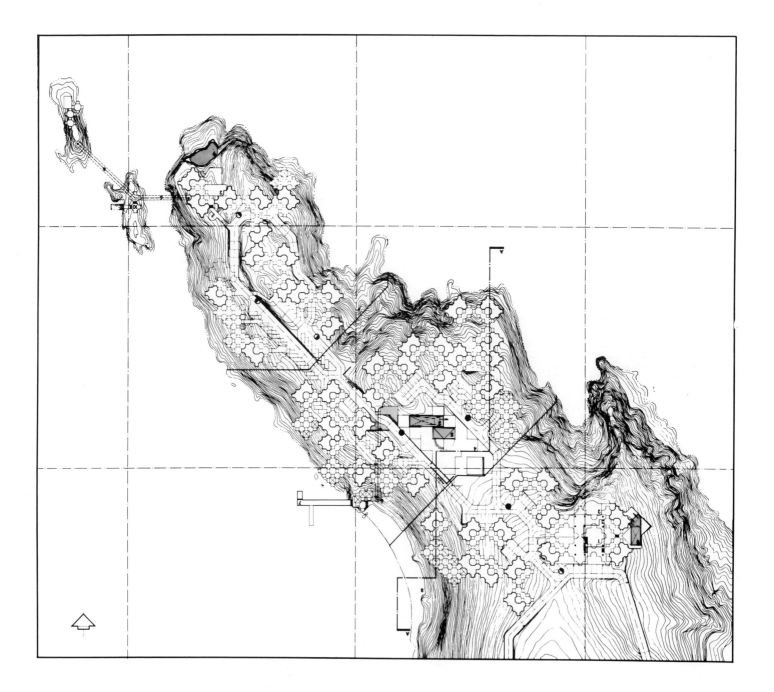

129. The site plan included 150 condominium units, a hotel, two beaches, and a recreation area, an island discotheque, and a minibus route.

130. A section through the site.

131. View of the rock cliffs from the sea.

132. View of the units from the sea. Model.

134. Tropaco. Detailed view of the cluster.

137. The cluster of rooms around the glazed courtyard forms a three-bedroom house with open patio for the condominium owner. When he is away, the house can be rented as four separate guest rooms with public access from the courtyard.

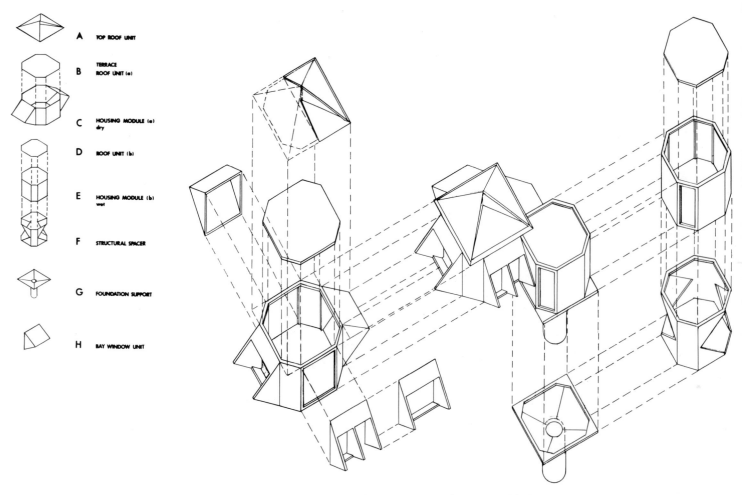

A TOP ROOF UNIT

B TERRACE
ROOF UNIT (a)

C HOUSING MODULE (a)
dry

D ROOF UNIT (b)

E HOUSING MODULE (b)
wet

F STRUCTURAL SPACER

G FOUNDATION SUPPORT

H BAY WINDOW UNIT

138. Exploded isometric showing the various components including shaded windows and ventilator roofs.

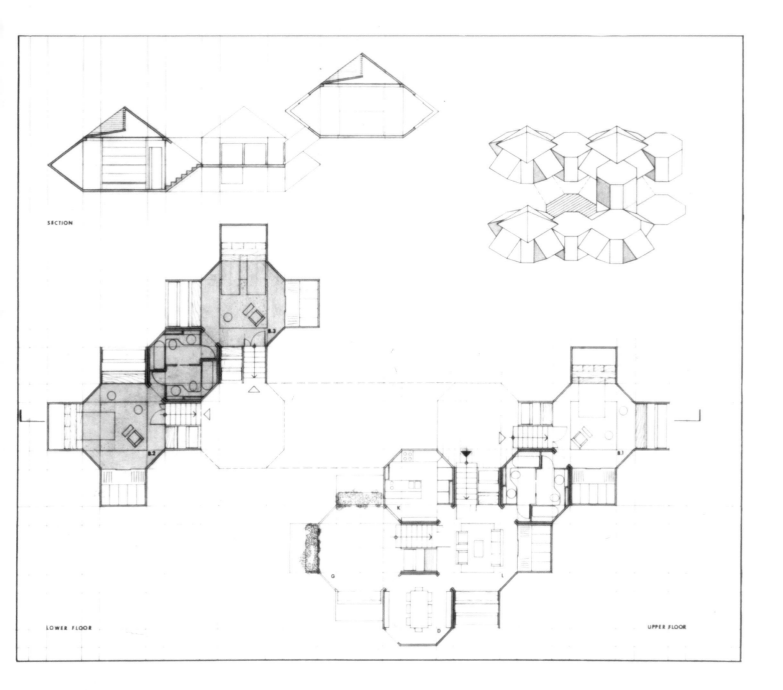

SECTION

LOWER FLOOR

UPPER FLOOR

## Indian Carry Resort,
## Saranac Lake, New York

This project consists of vacation home condominium units in a ski and lake resort area in northern New York. The housing units, based on the geometry of the rhombic dodecahedron, are built with wood panels clipped to a steel space frame. They require very small foundations and simple construction technology.

In all, there are to be 500 units, phased to be built over several years, clustered on the slopes in groups of 20 or 30, along with many recreation facilities such as a beach, tennis courts, ski trail, golf course, and marina.

Because of the remote location and scarcity of local labor, a prefabricated system was considered desirable, but not utilizing spatial elements, for ease of shipping. Pyramidical elements, consisting of four half-rhombic panels and incorporating structural framing and connectors, are shipped to the site nested inside one another. Six such elements would make up a complete module.

141. Model of the site plan, Saranac Lake, New York.

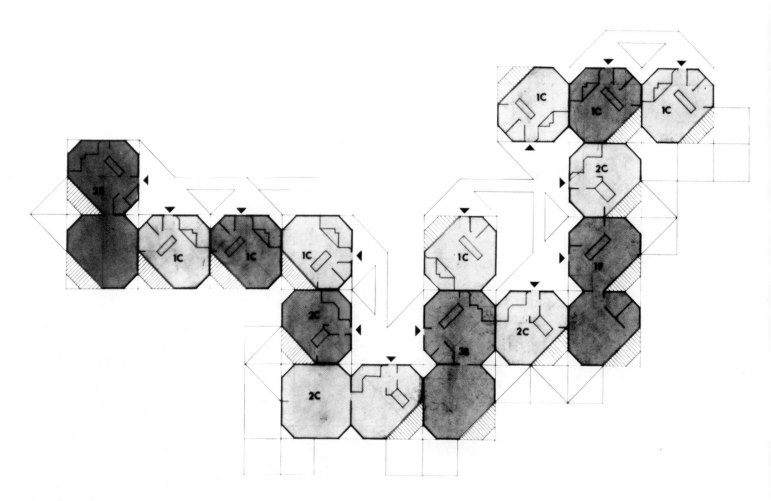

142. Plan of a typical cluster.

144. View of the cluster.

145. A single prototype built at North Hatley, Quebec.

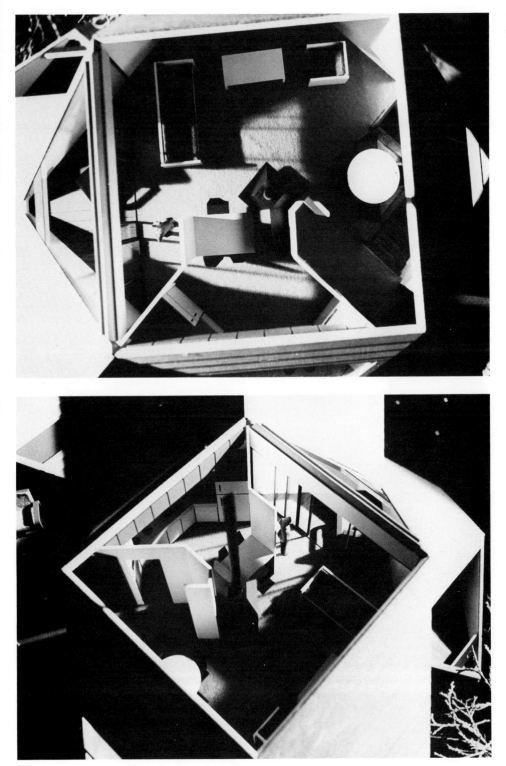

146, 147. Views of the living area of the typical module.

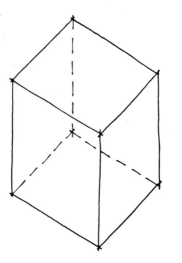

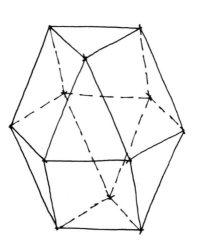

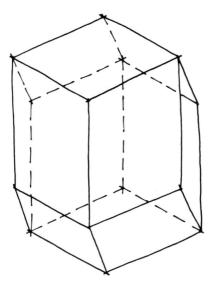

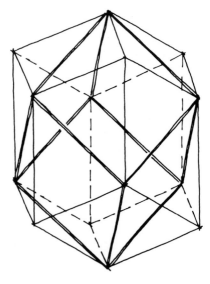

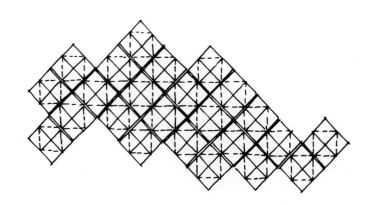

148. The geometry of the rhombic dodecahedron.

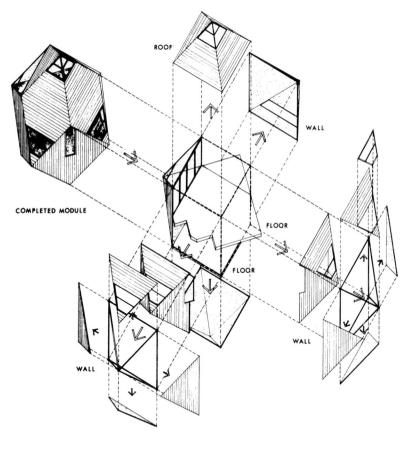

COMPLETED MODULE

ROOF

WALL

FLOOR

FLOOR

WALL

WALL

WALL

ASSEMBLY OF MODULE

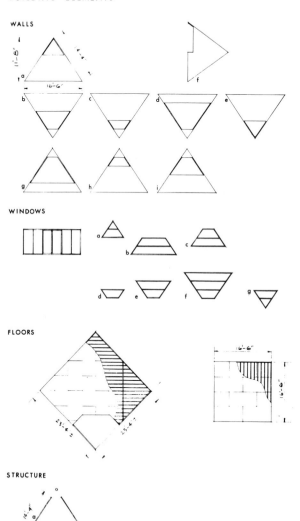

BUILDING ELEMENTS

WALLS

WINDOWS

FLOORS

STRUCTURE

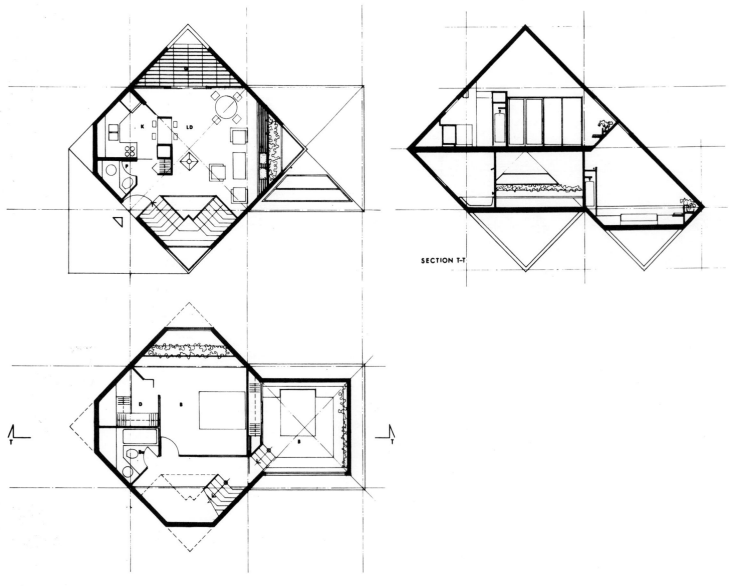

SECTION T-T

150. The two-bedroom unit with 768 square
feet of space.

151. Cross section showing construction
details.

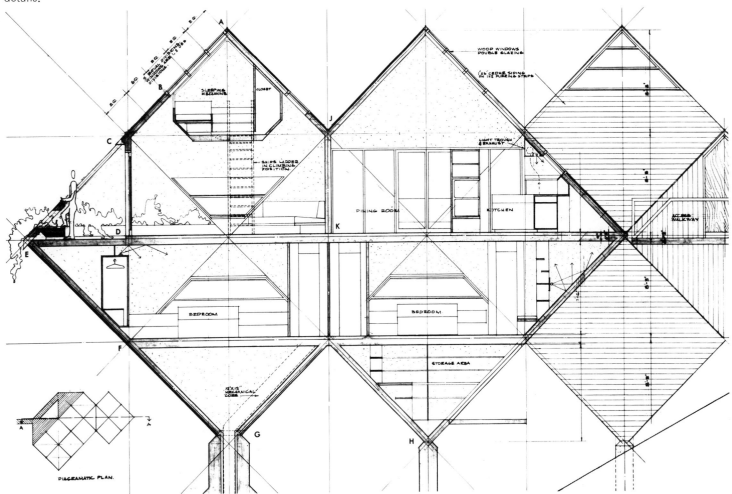

DIAGRAMATIC PLAN.

## Israel Habitat

In 1969 we were commissioned by the Ministry of Housing of the government of Israel to explore the possibility of applying sophisticated industrialized housing systems to government-sponsored housing. The plan was to establish one or two housing factories in strategic locations to supply sites in various parts of the country. Unlike Puerto Rico, the climatic conditions vary greatly from one part of the country to the other, from the cool mountain climate of the Jerusalem area, requiring heating and insulation, to the humid, hot climate of the plain, and the desert climate of the Negev. Greater versatility had to be achieved in the grouping of the units, the nature of the fenestration, and the technical details relating to heating, cooling, and insulation. The system also had to be adaptable to sites with varying topography and requiring different densities, from 10 to 40 dwelling units per acre, and from flat sites to hilly, rocky ones.

We devised a basic space cell that could adapt well to various densities, carpet housing two and three stories high, hillside clusters or terraced high-rise units. And we evolved the system of subcomponents which are additive to the basic space cell and which would respond to the varying climatic needs. Lightweight, insulated fiberglass domes were to extend the spaces of the houses in the mountainous area, to be replaced by more massive enclosures in desert locations.

Outdoor living is commonplace in Israel, but to respond to the hot summer sun or cool winter tenants enclose their terraces with readily available asbestos enclosures. We responded to this by developing a dome-shaped window and shutter that made the outdoor space instantly convertible from a shaded terrace on a sunny summer day to a roofless terrace on a cool summer evening to an enclosed greenhouse at wintertime.

The basic cluster consists of the modular units grouped in spiral formation around a vertical service stack that also accommodates service balconies for the kitchen. The clusters shelter parking below and are joined together by pedestrian bridges. The typical box is 12 feet wide and 38 feet long with a split-level at its two-thirds point. It was designed for construction with conventional concrete or with a chemically stressed lightweight concrete.

**Habitation**
162-163
**Israel Habitat**
**Variety of Densities**
**and Sites**

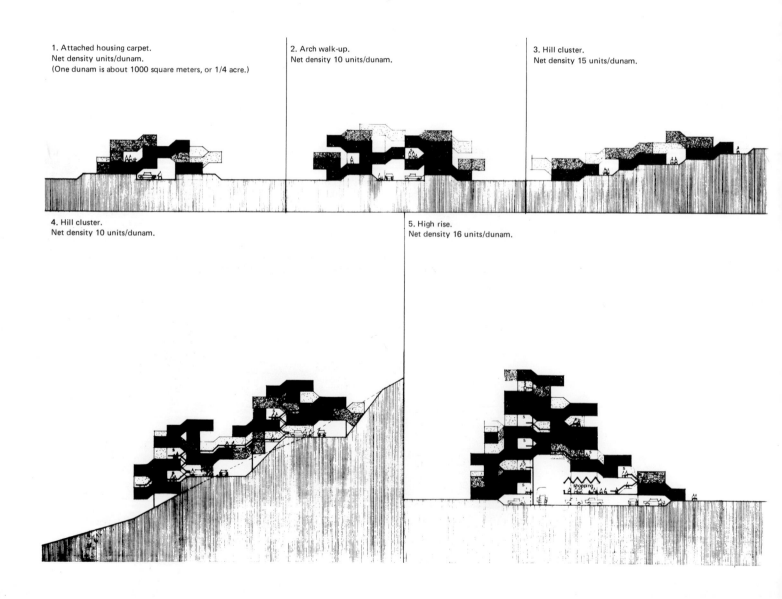

1. Attached housing carpet.
Net density units/dunam.
(One dunam is about 1000 square meters, or 1/4 acre.)

2. Arch walk-up.
Net density 10 units/dunam.

3. Hill cluster.
Net density 15 units/dunam.

4. Hill cluster.
Net density 10 units/dunam.

5. High rise.
Net density 16 units/dunam.

157. Hillside cluster forming first section of
Israel Habitat on Jerusalem site of Manchat.

159. The system is made up of concrete boxes and fiberglass domes.

160. View of the model showing the separation of roads and walkways.

161. The basic components of the system showing spiral formation and centrally located mechanical stack.

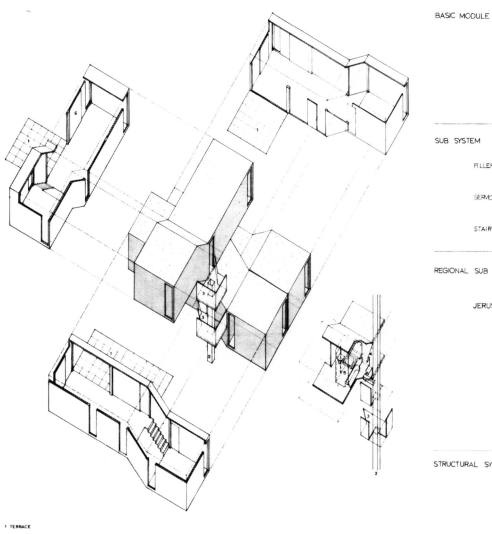

1 TERRACE

2 SHAFT

3 SERVICE   BALCONY

4 KITCHEN

5 BATHROOM

6 INSULATION

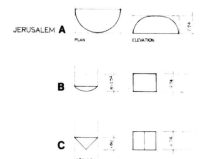

BASIC MODULE

PLAN

SECTION

SUB  SYSTEM

FILLER
PLAN          SECTION

SERVICE BALCONY

STAIRWAY

REGIONAL  SUB  SYSTEM

JERUSALEM **A**
PLAN          ELEVATION

**B**

**C**

STRUCTURAL  SYSTEM

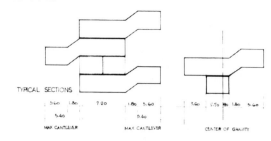

TYPICAL SECTIONS

MAX CANTILEVER          MAX CANTILEVER          CENTER OF GRAVITY

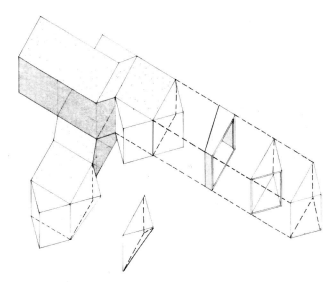

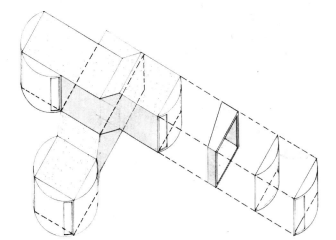

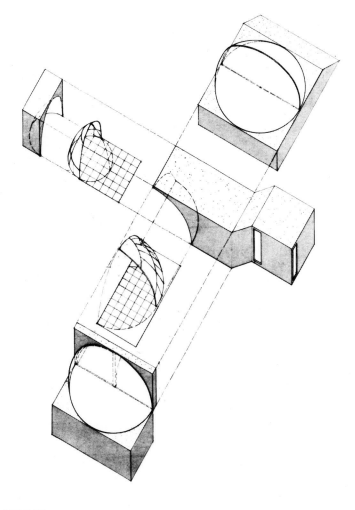

**A** JERUSALEM

**C**

**B**

**Habitation**
168-169
**Israel Habitat**
**Variations by the Addition**
**of Subcomponents**

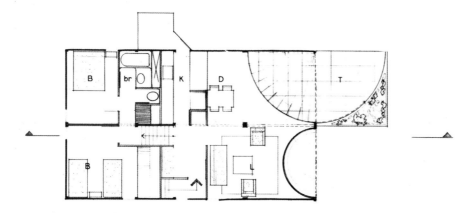

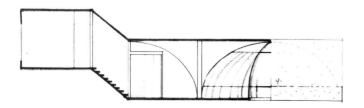

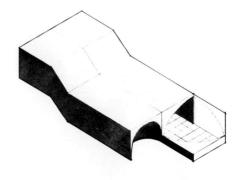

**A II 3**
| | |
|---|---|
| Inside area | 77 m² |
| 50% Covered terrace | 5 |
| Gross area incl walls | 82 |
| Open roof terrace | 10 |

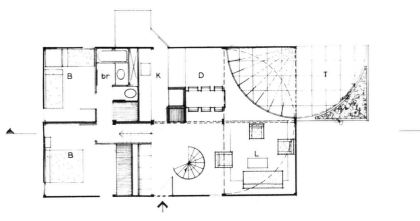

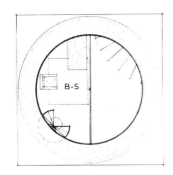

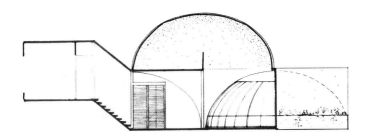

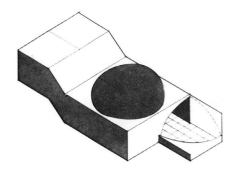

**A III 3**

| | |
|---|---|
| Inside area | 95 m² |
| 50% Covered terrace | 5 |
| Gross area incl. walls | 100 |
| Open roof terrace | 10 |

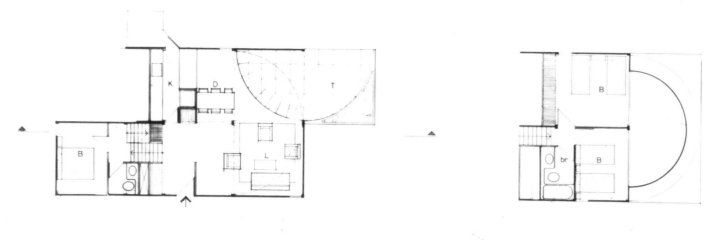

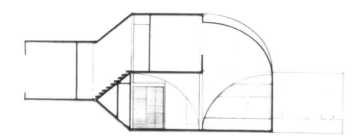

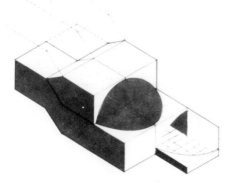

**A III 1**

| | |
|---|---|
| Inside area | 97 m² |
| 50% Covered terrace | 5 |
| Gross area incl. walls | 102 |
| Open roof terrace | 10 |

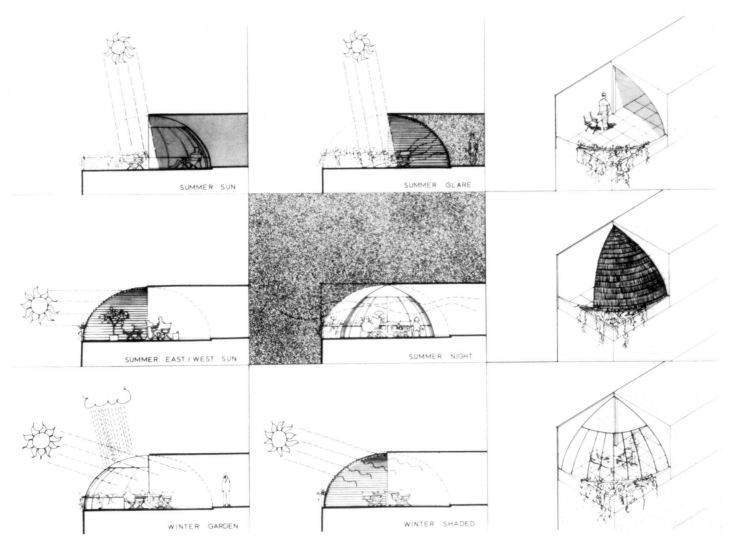

SUMMER SUN

SUMMER GLARE

SUMMER EAST/WEST SUN

SUMMER NIGHT

WINTER GARDEN

WINTER SHADED

170. A rotating 1/4-dome allows the garden
areas to be used to best advantage all year
round.

Working with the Community

In Puerto Rico, I was invited to prepare plans by a developer who, while working in cooperation with a government agency, Fomento Cooporativo, was nevertheless acting as a business corporation apart from the community.

In Israel, it was the Ministry of Housing that asked me to develop the plans. But the Ministry, while it is a public agency, did not afford any contact or communication with anyone who might live in the projects that were being considered.

However, both in Rochester and Baltimore the situation is fundamentally different. We have contact with the people who might be members of the new community. In the case of Rochester, the FIGHT group sponsoring the cooperative includes in its membership many people who may live in the project. In the case of Baltimore, the community group with which we have been working from the outset is made up of several neighborhood organizations representing people who live around the site, and groups like the Cylburn Wildflower and Garden Preserve Association and the Citizens' Planning and Housing Association that represent city-wide interests. They look at Coldspring as a place which might affect their lives and about which they have something to say.

We also have continuous contact with the mayor and his office, with the Planning Commission, with the Housing Department (the client), with the Board of Education, with the Welfare Department, with the hospitals that might provide medical services on the site, with the public library system of Baltimore. Each of these community or public authorities is involved in the process, not only at the level of how a house might be designed or what the grouping of houses will be but with what the social fabric of this particular community should be.

But is the physical design of the Rochester project really fundamentally different from Israel Habitat or Puerto Rico Habitat? I think not. But the way in which it is being built, the fact that the modular factory might be owned by the community, the fact that the people who live there might be working in that factory, the fact that we might be getting federal grants to train people for work in the plant, and that the FIGHT group might sponsor the businesses and the day-care facility in the neighborhood center make it a much more meaningful undertaking. The people who will move into Puerto Rico Habitat or Israel Habitat will see it as housing provided by the government.

I'll never forget the two days when sixty members of the FIGHT group came in two busloads to Montreal. On the evening of their arrival, we met at the Holiday Inn and had dinner together. Most of them were saying, "We don't want high-density housing, we don't want anything that has elevators. What we really want are town houses; we've had enough of high-rise housing." And then on Saturday and Sunday, slowly, as we walked through Habitat and into the houses and out onto the terraces, they began to say, "Yes, we would like to live in this kind of place. But can we afford it?" Which was really what the issue was in the first place, as I saw it.

It would be pretentious to say that the physical design of houses or building systems has been greatly influenced by the community meetings. I had hoped that it would be, but this has not happened. But it is also true that the whole image of the community both in my eyes and theirs has been totally changed by the fact that they are part of the planning process. In terms of the future quality of a living community, that is a very fundamental difference.

## Rochester Habitat

Rochester Habitat is to be a residential community for families with low and moderate incomes. The site is approximately 30 acres divided into three sections along the Genesee River in the Third Ward Renewal Project, Rochester, New York.

A series of internal service roads, linked to the major city street at four locations, lead directly to the parking facilities and also provide access with sufficient headroom for delivery, garbage, and fire trucks, and the like. Pedestrian paths never cross this network on grade. Instead, pedestrians use a walkway one and one-half floors above the parking level. This walk runs continuously through the entire site, linking all the dwelling units, shopping, and community facilities. In the taller clusters, there are additional walkways every second floor which give access to the dwellings themselves. These are served by elevators and fire stairs.

Because the budget was so strict, the size of the dwelling unit is, by general agreement, minimal. We tried to plan the units so that they would have a feeling of spaciousness, even though they were small in floor area. The living spaces open out to a terrace through sliding glass doors. A sloped roof element allows greater height in the living room and provides a view of the upper floor volume (which is the bedroom area). Residents are given the option of sheltering or enclosing the terrace for winter use. The railing system for the terraces is designed so that the addition of a simple inclined transparent or opaque roof makes it possible for the tenant to enclose the space for himself.

172. View of the site of the project from the river. Winter scene.

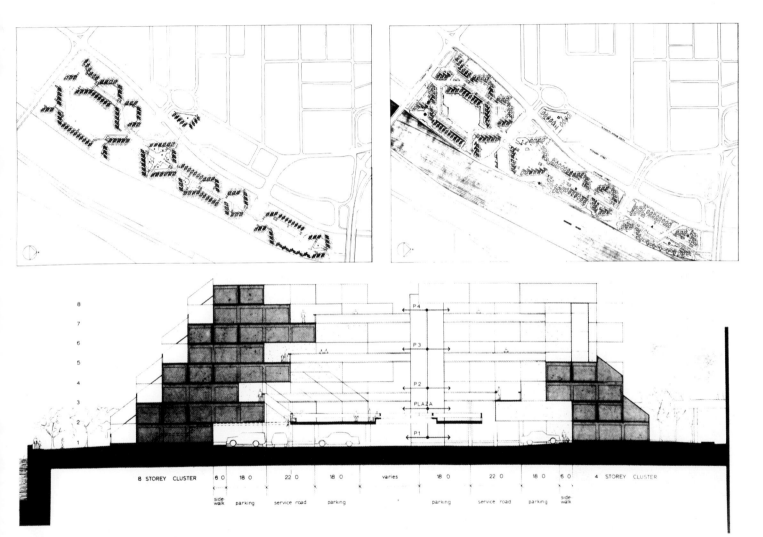

175. Site plan—pedestrian level.

176. Site plan—vehicular level.

177. A section through the site.

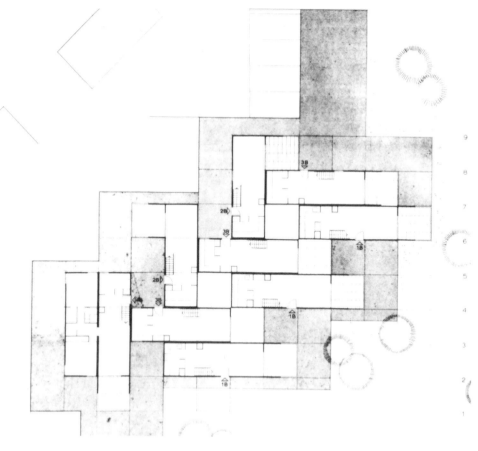

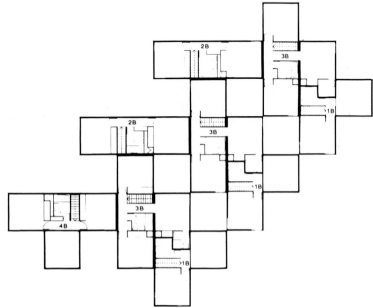

178-181. Plans of a typical four-story cluster.

178. Ground-floor access level with private gardens.

179. Second floor, bedrooms and baths only.

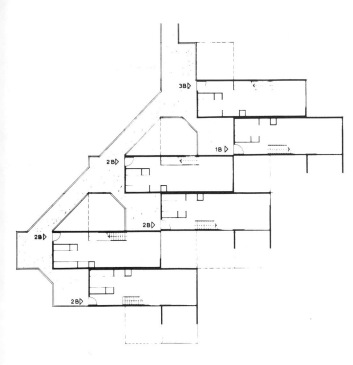

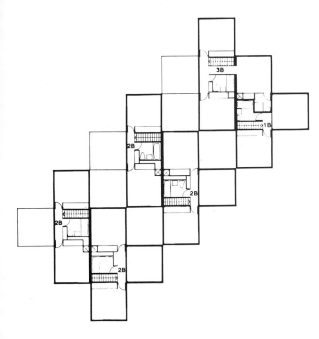

180. Third floor, access to upper units.

181. Fourth floor, bedroom level.

12-0
12-0
12-0

MBR 120

**IB**  UPPER LEVEL

MBR 120

BR2 125

**2B**  TYPE 1  UPPER LEVEL

12-0
12-0
12-0

D/L 240

K60

**IB**  AREA 605 S.F.
LOWER LEVEL

D/L 240

K 60

**2B**  AREA 800 S.F.
TYPE 1  LOWER LEVEL

12-0    12-0    12-0

12-0    12-0    12-0

**3B** TYPE 1 UPPER LEVEL

BR2 100
MBR 125
BR3 110

**3B** TYPE 2 UPPER LEVEL

BR2 120
MBR 125
BR3 125

**3B** AREA 975 S.F
TYPE 1 LOWER LEVEL

L 170
K 60
D 116
T

**3B** AREA 975 S.F
TYPE 2 LOWER LEVEL

D/L 240
K 80
T

12'-0"    12'-0"    12'-0"          12'-0"    12'-0"    12'-0"

## Coldspring New Town, Baltimore, Maryland

In 1971, we were commissioned by the city of Baltimore to develop a master plan and building plans for the new community of Coldspring. The site, located 10 minutes from downtown Baltimore, comprised 500 acres of which 200 acres are the wildlife preserve of Cylburn Park. The 300 developable acres consisted mostly of sloping land heavily treed and a large quarry rising 250 feet from its pit. The site is surrounded by many communities: the main city, Druid Hill Park to the south, the Park Heights Community in northwest Baltimore to the west consisting mostly of lower- and lower-middle-income families, the Mount Washington area and Cross Keys development to the north and east consisting mostly of upper-middle and luxury accommodations, and a lower-middle-income area to the southeast. The scope of the project posed problems at many levels.

First, to involve all the communities surrounding the site with their different and sometimes contradictory interests in the design and realization process of the town so that they could identify with its execution and benefit from its development. Second, to create a community that has enough of its own identity with its own institutional and community services to attract families who have the choice and now opt for living outside city limits. And at the same time, to make it part of the continuous fabric of the city around it rather than a fenced-off enclave.

Third, to find the technical means of building moderate-density housing on the sloping terrain, taking full advantage of the site features within the economic constraints set by the program. Fourth, to construct a variety of housing types ranging in density and cost so that they would respond to the needs of families of various size and incomes. Fifth, to reexamine basic city services—the school system, the health system, park and recreation facilities—and to be as innovative in providing attractive services and institutions on the site as one is about the physical plant.

To respond to this rather ambitious program, the city decided simultaneously with the commissioning of the planning and design team to retain developers to work with this team so that all aspects of the development and design process would be considered. The Rouse-Wates group was selected to join forces with the planning team to develop a complete and detailed master plan and preliminary building plans for the city's approval.

186. Aerial view of part of the Coldspring site with the Jonesfalls Expressway in the foreground. The quarry can be seen on the left.

188. Coldspring New Town, indicating open space system, residential area, the town center, neighborhood centers, schools, and the office and research and development space.

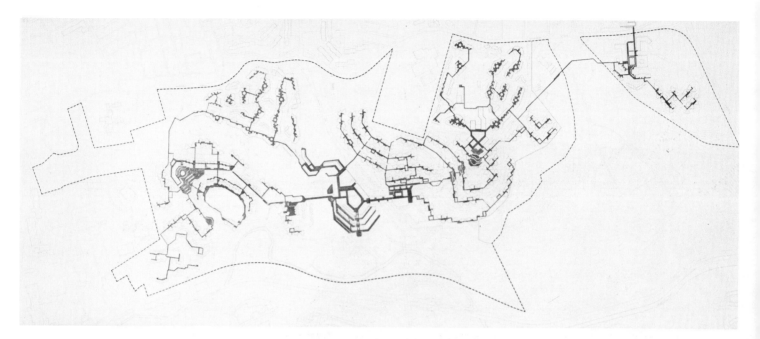

189. Coldspring New Town pedestrian
system.

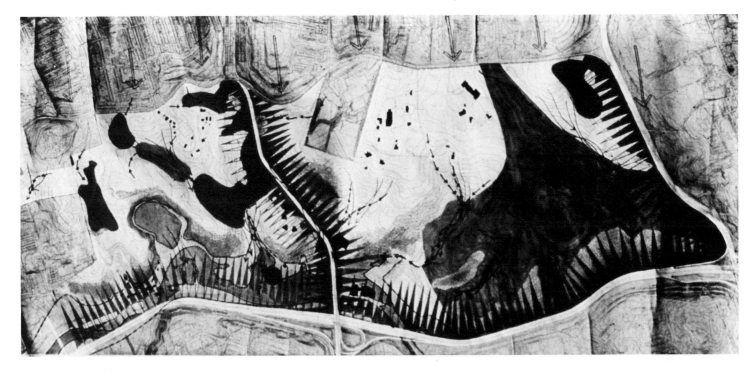

190. Analysis of site characteristics.

### 191. The Town Center

Spanning Cold Spring Lane with a shopping bridge and accommodating 100,000 square feet of community shopping, 400,000 square feet of rental office space including a municipal service building, community facilities, clinics, a little school, and other services. It connects the two halves of the site on either side of Cold Spring Lane and is serviced by four levels of deck parking below.

The town center extends in the form of the pedestrian spine northward and southward toward the two neighborhood centers above the quarry and at the northern extremity of the site.

Parking was restricted to centralized locations, the rest of the site being served by an internal minibus system. An overall gross density of 15 units to the acre was established.

192. View of the town center from the north.

**Habitation**
192-193
**Coldspring New Town**
**Deck Housing**

193. Low-density decked housing. A mixture of town houses and maisonnette units served by a pedestrian deck, with parking and services below, results in a density of 23 units to the acre.

194. Section of deck houses at center of group.

195. Section of deck houses at end of group.

196. Plan view at deck level.

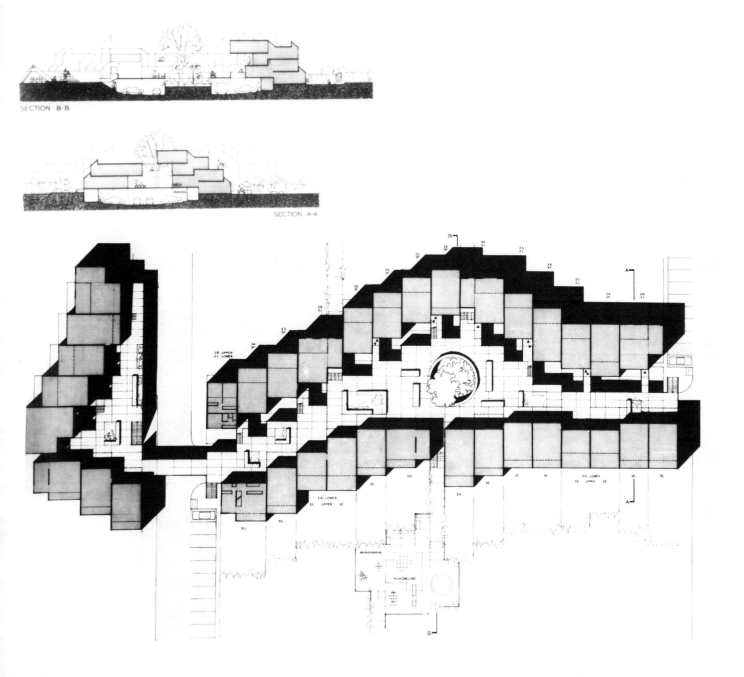

SECTION B-B

SECTION A-A

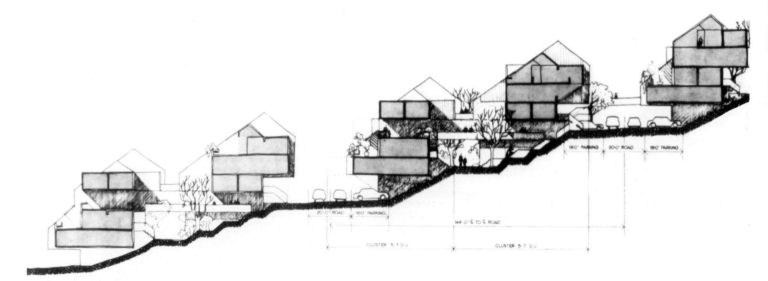

197. Section through cluster houses.

199. Cluster housing: detail of the model showing the clusters, the driveway, parking, and pedestrian walkways.

200. Cluster housing. The parking and driveway occur every two clusters, and serve downwards with a secondary pedestrian greenway occurring on grade between the two subclusters. The contract for the project explicitly stated that each housing type be investigated for various construction methods, to determine the most economical and attractive procedure.

201. Detailed view of the cluster housing.

**Habitation**
**198-199**
**Coldspring New Town**
**Housing in the Quarry**

202. Housing in the quarry. Units are grouped down the quarry cliffs with entrances from the top descending twenty-five stories to the lake formed at its pit. The quarry forms a horseshoe with the units looking out of the aperture toward the city forming their own internal environment of their recreational lake at the bottom.

203. The quarry.

204. General view of quarry housing from the lake.

# 3

## BUILDING IN THE FACTORY

Unless we find ways of assembling large components with the simplicity of slapping mortar between two bricks, then the advantages of factory-made components, which seem to be obvious to anyone, are overwhelmed by the new problems.

We take for granted that it makes sense to industrialize building. The quality control we can have and the reduction of labor input are obvious advantages of the assembly line. But if we expect to achieve a radical reduction of costs, we are likely to be disappointed. With all the efficiencies of assembly-line techniques, we might cut the cost of labor by one-third. (The cost of materials, half the total cost, doesn't go down.) This has to be offset by a fairly appreciable capitalization for special equipment. So we are talking about a cost reduction of less than 15 percent, not a very significant amount.

But there are very real advantages to industrialization that aren't directly related to cost. One is the possibility of a management structure and a scale of capital investment that would permit a continuous process of research and development. It would also support major tooling-up costs, which could be amortized over a reasonable period of time. The research and development that have taken place in other industries have, over time, transformed products like the airplane and the radio. We don't even know what improvements might take place in the construction industry.

The irony of Habitat 67, Puerto Rico Habitat, and the project in Rochester is that they are being executed in the fragmented, disorganized structure of the industry as it exists today. They are being done by private contractors and subcontractors with little contact with the manufacturing industries that supply them. Research and development of new techniques have been limited to those small innovations that can be conceived and initiated by our team and our consultants, such as novel structural details or joints, and to those of our clients who are restricted by limited resources. We are basically working out of Sweet's Catalogue (a ten-volume catalogue of standard architectural materials and components), and any pretentions of anything else are really a farce.

What we are doing is developing the systematic physical attributes of a system that could lend itself to real industrial production if our client was manufacturing 5000 units a year in a large plant with experienced labor, and if he had a technical staff researching new materials and generating design data based on production experience. In that situation, we could set problems for suppliers, and the suppliers would take them seriously because they'd be dealing with a quantity purchaser buying components for 5000 or 10,000 or even 100,000 units a year. No corporation like that exists now.

Talking about the need to industrialize in 1963 was a kind of far-out fantasy. Today government programs like Operation Breakthrough are set up to encourage it; there's no debate. But it hasn't begun to happen.

Merely to say "it's not happening" and leave it at that would suggest that the industry is infested with nasty, cigar-smoking men who want nothing but to make money in the old time-tested way and idealistic-looking, flag-waving architects, planners, and community groups who want nothing but to have a good environment. The situation is obviously more complex. There are fundamental things about the housing business that are obstacles to industrialization. When we talk about marketing cars or airplanes or toasters, we are talking about a predictable market. This is not true of buildings; no one can figure out who will want them, or where, in any systematic way. Therefore, the investments in tooling-up, in research and design, are risky. The only areas where this is beginning to be overcome are in the cases where a particular authority controls part of the market, such as schools. We have school systems emerging because that market has been easier to aggregate.

Another problem for large-scale production is that building codes and zoning laws are different across the country. Many details are affected by codes, ranging from the type of connection between electrical wires, or whether a window can be located under a cantilever, to fireproofing. All these affect the basic design of a system, and to find one prototype that will satisfy all of them is not easy.

Still another problem is that most manufactured items are relatively compact, and therefore nationwide distribution is feasible. For instance, a car or a refrigerator might cost $15 per cubic foot, but a house costs only $3 per cubic foot, so distribution and packaging are a much costlier part of the whole process. Consequently, the marketing radius of any one plant is limited.

Then there are the logistical problems of "hardware." When you join two I beams, by welding or riveting, it's pretty simple. But when you take two 30-ton space cells and try to connect them, the techniques we have developed up to now don't work very well.

It's not that we haven't done these things in other industries. We've got fireproof plastics that are used in the nose cones of rockets. We've learned to manufacture large components of sheet metal for aircraft to incredibly precise tolerances; and we've learned to connect the hydraulic and electrical assemblies in aircraft with great versatility. But all that is quite meaningless when one talks about a product on which we already spend 20 percent of our personal income at a rate of about $3 per cubic foot. If we spent $15 per cubic foot, five times as much, it would consume a family's entire earnings.

The General Housing Corporation is nonexistent yet; that fantastically efficient, integrated process of management, building, and marketing of housing does not exist. So the step-by-step pictures of the assembly line for Habitat 67 or Puerto Rico must be viewed as a crude and primitive beginning. They are both limited-size, partially handmade prototypes. They were built on limited production lines in which some of the techniques and design problems of space-cell construction were exposed and explored.

The general problems of industrialized building, and the problems of building with space cells in particular, such as occur when you take boxes and lift them into place with a crane, are inherent in the use of three-dimensional modules.

But when boxes are offset and cantilevered to form gardens or have openings on all four sides, this creates problems that are the result of a particular environmental concept.

When I was commissioned by Development International Corporation to design Puerto Rico Habitat, it was not clear to them that there was a difference between the concept of building with factory-produced boxes and building a Habitat design. They liked Habitat. But as we started to detail the design, and a typical hillside cluster was evolved, they began to see some of the special problems. For example, the roof terraces have to be surfaced in such a way that water will not seep into the dwelling below. We wanted openings in the long walls of the module, a feature that meant extra reinforcing bars and more complicated molds. They were included in the design out of a conviction that they are important to a good living environment.

So when, after two years of working with us, our client was approached by the Housing Corporation of America (a subsidiary of Alcoa), with the suggestion that they use the Habitat box system to build two- and three-story town houses, our client discovered that half the problems he had been dealing with were not a direct result of building with boxes but the result of the Habitat design. It is much easier to accept as design criterion that the plumbing stack should run straight through a building vertically, with a maximum number of kitchens and bathrooms hooked to it than to say, "I want to group the units in space so that each has a garden and privacy and sunlight and a particular kind of entrance, and still have the plumbing line up." But that is essentially what we're trying to do.

What do we mean when we use the word "technology"? Lightness, new materials, energy conservation, rapid construction, adaptability, and flexibility—those are the words that come to mind. The work I am doing is built within the limited means of immediately available technology, not only constrained by the availability of certain materials but further constrained by the economics of the day and even further by prevailing codes and practices. These are tight confines that I might be able to modify, but only slightly. Bubbles hanging on cables and mile-long masts connected by tubes that recirculate energy resources and liquids, completely powered by magic solar batteries, are attractive thoughts, but I know very surely that if I hope to build today or in the near future then they are not immediate options. The technological progress we've made is modest. The Montreal Habitat box weighed 70 tons, because of its size (which was 38 feet by 17 feet), and its 5-inch slabs and walls. The walls were thick because we had to get a 4-hour fire rating, and this meant a 2-inch cover of concrete on either side of 1 inch of the reinforcing steel. In Puerto Rico, the wall is 3 1/2 inches thick, enough cover to meet the local fire code. At the same time, it is the minimum we could go to and still cover our reinforcing bars adequately. The Puerto Rico box itself is smaller, and we are using lightweight concrete with a lightweight aggregate. In all, the box has been reduced in weight to about 25 tons. The next step is easy to project. A material that weighs 50 pounds per cubic foot (one-third of the weight of conventional concrete and half that of lightweight concrete) and that has sufficient strength to be used in a 3-inch wall would give a module weighing less than 10 tons. And at that point, you have a product that can be hoisted by conventional equipment without much problem. Then a building system of three-dimensional modules becomes formidable economic competition with the other techniques widely used today. That means more capital will be invested in sophisticated production equipment, research, and development. Then perhaps we can start to develop new products or building systems that respond much more sensitively to our changing needs: inexpensive mechanized or pneumatic movable walls, windows that operate like the iris of the eye, furniture that you leave behind when you move.

One of the most intriguing changes we learned to make in the process of design for factory construction was in the preparation of drawings for Habitat 67. Instead of architectural working drawings of the complete structure, we made foldout assembly drawings of each type of box and indicated its location in the structure in a small key "map."

For Puerto Rico Habitat, Conrad Engineers developed a computer program that could analyze the stresses in each box and then draw the reinforcing pattern that would take that stress. They are much more like shop drawings than regular architectural documents. And within the module drawings, numbers indicate the location of preassembled subcomponents, kitchen K-8 for example, or bathroom B-10.

With interchangeable subcomponents or standard "chassis" we could achieve incredible complexity and variety of spaces through the design of the "map," without overloading the production system at all.

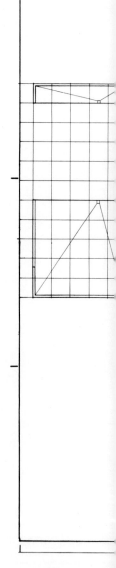

1. Typical foldout plan of the modular unit
as drawn in the construction documents.

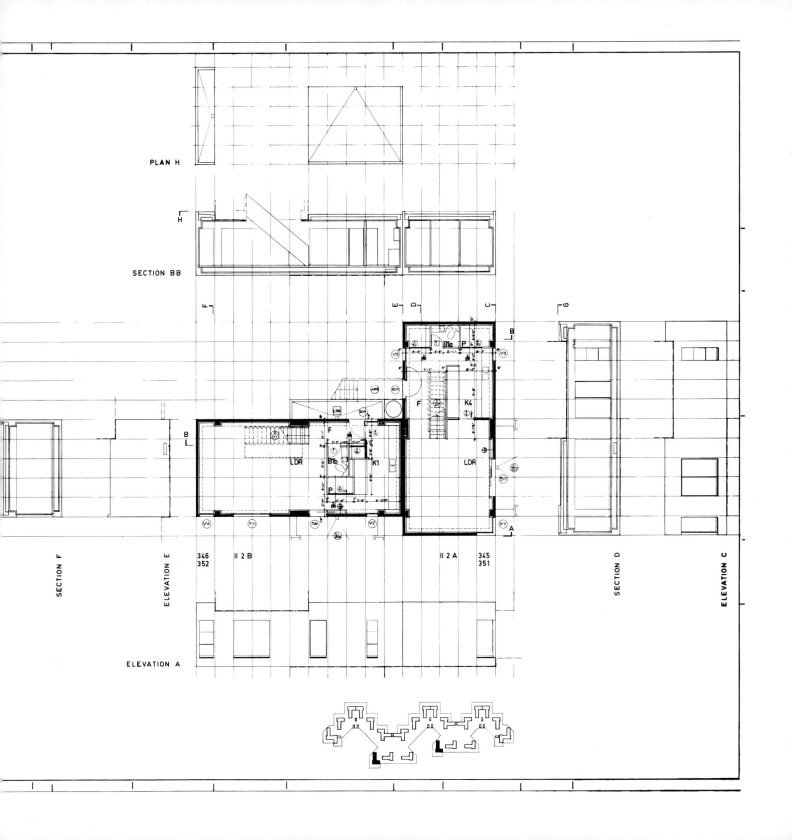

PLAN H

SECTION BB

SECTION F

ELEVATION E

SECTION D

ELEVATION C

346
352

II 2 B

II 2 A

345
351

ELEVATION A

LDR

LDR

B1a

B1b

K1

K4

P

P

F

F

2-7. Computer printouts of Puerto Rico Habitat cluster structural analysis. The computer graphically plots shear and bending stresses, horizontal and vertical deflection, and responding reinforcing patterns. The analysis of the cluster by computer was made possible through the development of a special program by Conrad Engineers, New York.

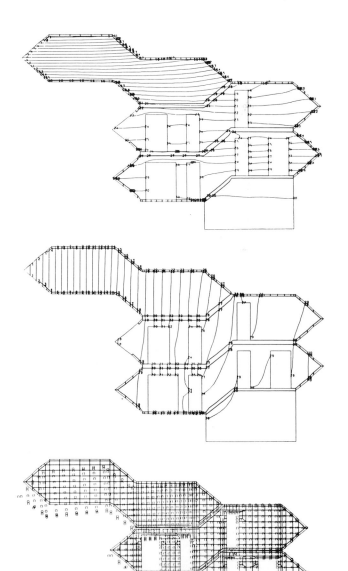

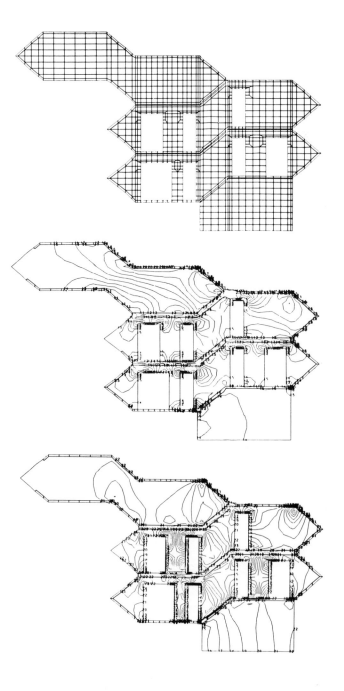

8. Reinforcing drawing for the typical module.
9. Standardized welded mesh panels for the typical module.

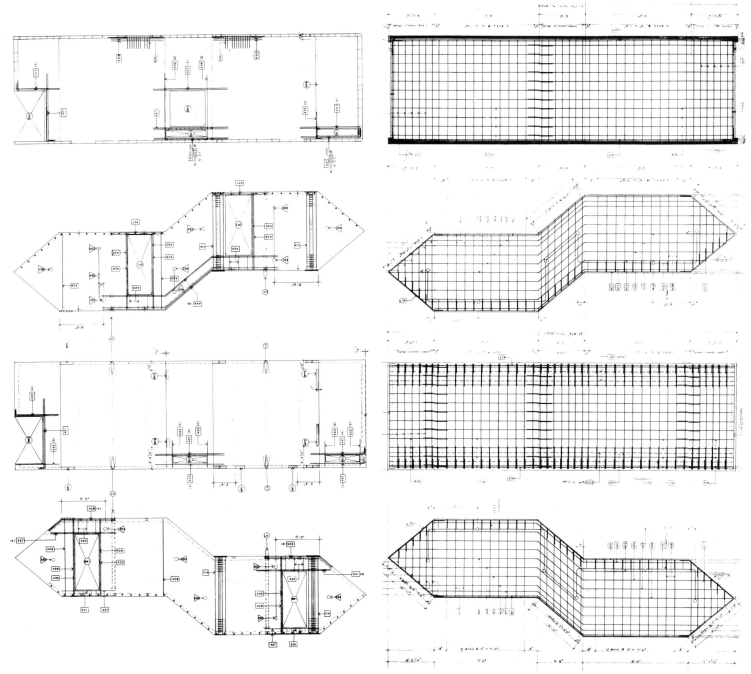

Steel reinforcing rod
stock piles

The factory

Housing modules waiting
to be hoisted

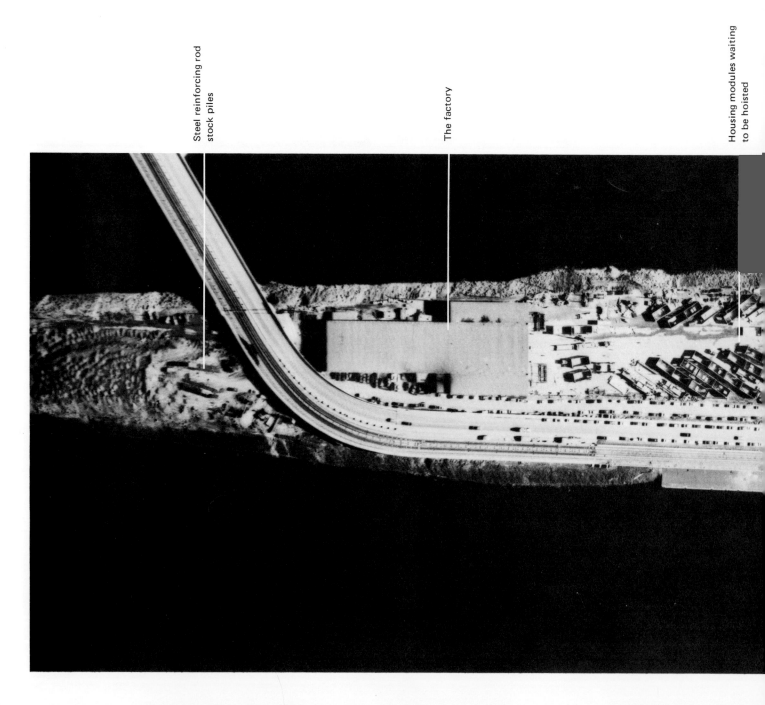

The stiffleg derrick crane

Accessory precast elements and roofs

Fire stair and elevator shaft precast sections

11. Preparing the site for Habitat 67.

12. Driving piles.

13. The lower-level parking structure is cast
in place.

14. Making the box, preparing the reinforcing panels.

15. Assembling the reinforcing steel cage.

16. Moving the cage into the molds.

17. Placing the inner molds.

18. Pouring concrete into the molds.

19. Pouring the floor slabs.

20. Steam curing of the concrete module.

21. The stripped module with its temporary polyethelene roof is moved to the assembly line.

22. The typical post-tensioning and connection details between boxes.

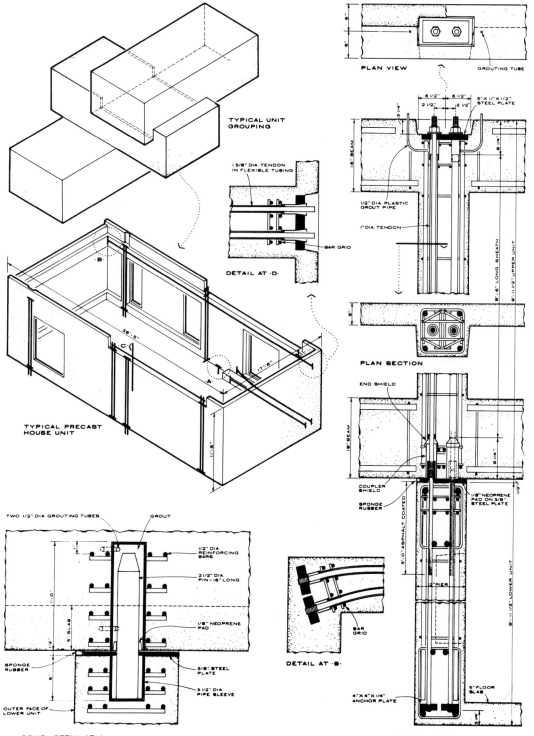

TYPICAL UNIT
GROUPING

1 3/8" DIA. TENDON
IN FLEXIBLE TUBING

DETAIL AT ·D·

BAR GRID

TYPICAL PRECAST
HOUSE UNIT

PLAN VIEW

GROUTING TUBE

6 1/2"   6 1/2"
2 1/2"   2 1/2"
5" X 11" X 1/2"
STEEL PLATE

18" BEAM

1/2" DIA. PLASTIC
GROUT PIPE

1" DIA. TENDON

9'-6" LONG SHEATH

9'-11 1/2" UPPER UNIT

PLAN SECTION

END SHIELD

18" BEAM

COUPLER
SHIELD

SPONGE
RUBBER

3'-0" ASPHALT COATED

1/8" NEOPRENE
PAD ON 3/8"
STEEL PLATE

PIER

9'-11 1/2" LOWER UNIT

4" X 4" X 1/4"
ANCHOR PLATE

5" FLOOR
SLAB

VERTICAL SECTION AT ·C·
(TENDON DETAIL)

TWO 1/2" DIA GROUTING TUBES     GROUT

1/2" DIA
REINFORCING
BARS

2 1/2" DIA
PIN-18" LONG

1/8" NEOPRENE
PAD

SPONGE
RUBBER

3/8" STEEL
PLATE

3 1/2" DIA
PIPE SLEEVE

OUTER FACE OF
LOWER UNIT

DOWEL DETAIL AT ·A·

BAR
GRID

DETAIL AT ·B·

23. The finishing crews install insulation inside the module.

24. The assembly line—installing the windows.

25. Panels of wood flooring are installed and sanded.

26. Following the installation of plasterboard over the insulation, the interior is painted. Then the modular electrical baseboard is placed.

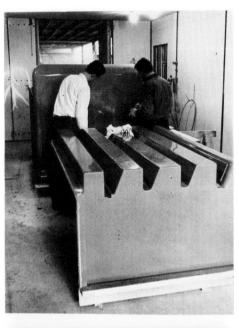

27. Manufacturing the molds for making the fiberglass bathroom.

28. The prefabricated fiberglass bathroom being hoisted into the box.

29. The piping and wiring assembly is completed in the factory.

30. Detail of the interior of the fiberglass bathroom showing the gel-coat finish of the sink, counter, medicine cabinet, and the tub.

31. Plan and sections of the typical bathroom.

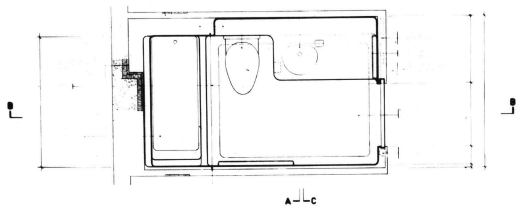

A ⌐ C

PLAN

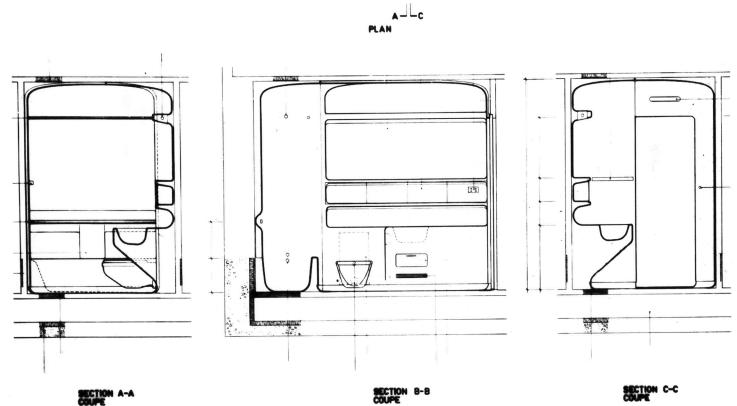

SECTION A-A
COUPE

SECTION B-B
COUPE

SECTION C-C
COUPE

32. The custom-built stiff-leg derrick crane lifts the 70-ton prefinished box into place.

33. The crane at work hoisting the boxes into place in the south cluster.

34. The roof being lifted into place. The flags are to celebrate the hoisting of last unit.

36. The precast pedestrian street sections waiting in line to be hoisted into place.

37. The precast pedestrian street section forming one-half of the total box girder being hoisted into place.

38. The stairs are formed of repetitive three-dimensional precast sections.

39. The post tensioning of the street girder showing the sixteen 500-kip cables in the process of tensioning. (One kip is 1000 pounds.)

40. Boxes in place, the roof garden decks and planters are installed.

**Building in the Factory**
226-227
**Building Habitat 67
Habitat Infrastructure,
Pedestrian Streets and
Mechanical Services**

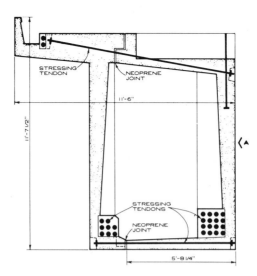

SECTION THRU GIRDER

41, 44. Diagram showing the cross section through the street girder with the longitudinal and lateral post-tensioning cables. The pattern of the post-tensioning cables follows the catenary curve of the stress distribution.

45. Section and plan view of the mechanical street, showing the arrangements of the pipes and wires and their distribution from the elevator core to the mechanical shaft.

42. Interior view of the pedestrian street, showing the mechanical distribution tunnel with the drainage, sewer, hot water, and electrical distribution system.

43. One-half of the street girder in place.

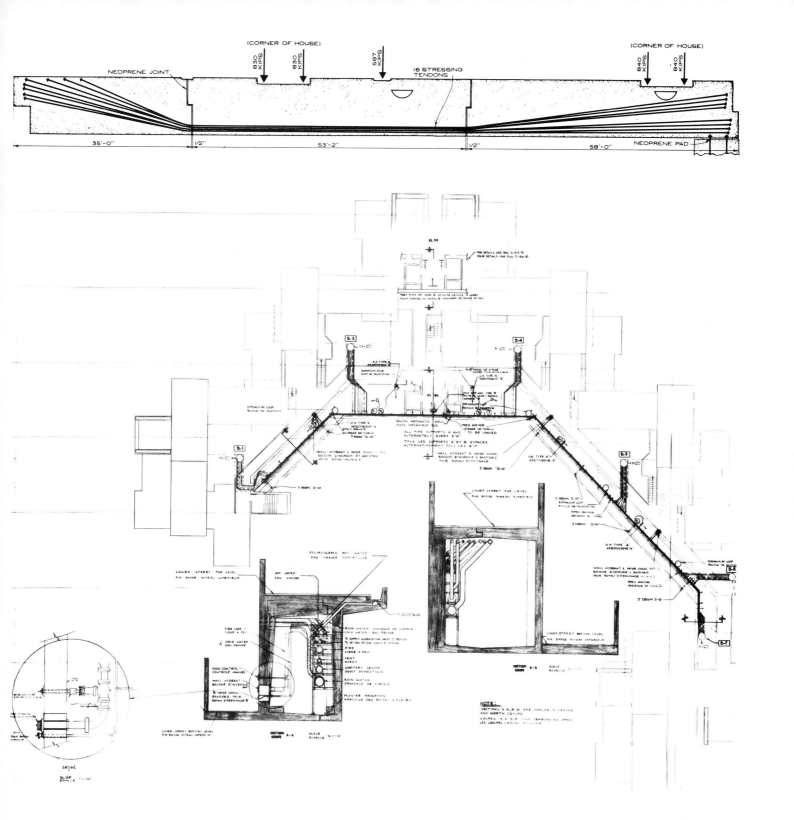

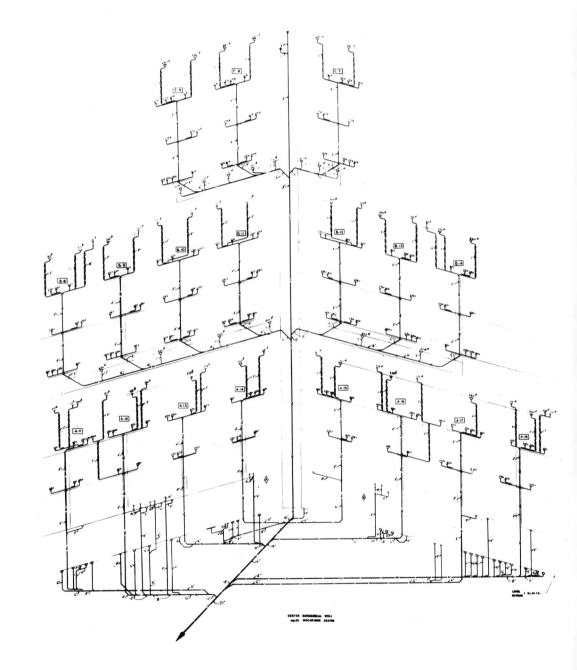

46. The plumbing diagram.

47. The electrical distribution pattern.

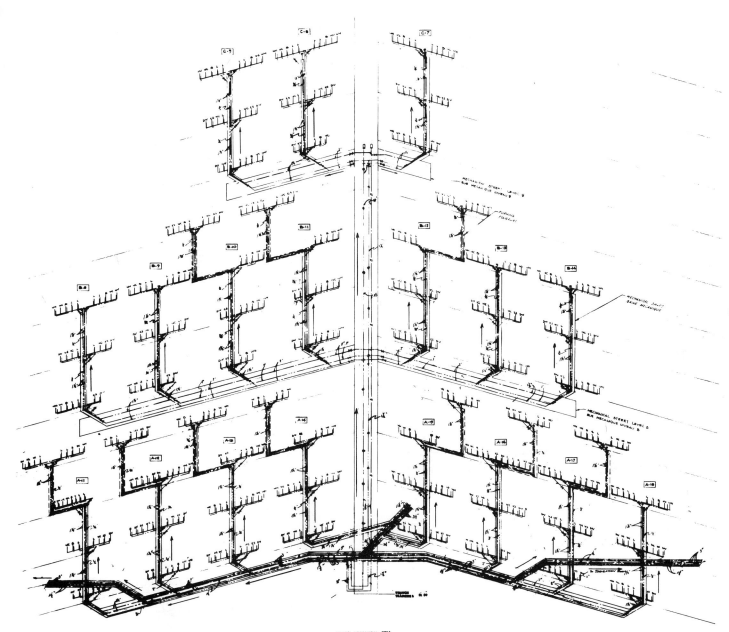

48. Detail view of the subfloor space within the module.

49. The fan coil unit that is located under the subfloor and acts as heater and air conditioner for the typical modular box of 600 square feet.

50. View of the boiler room supplying heating and hot water for the entire complex.

51. The mechanical distribution shaft with its cover removed, showing the drainage pipes, hot and cold water distribution, electrical conduits, and electrical boxes. The cover of the shaft is made with insulated gelcoated fiberglass.

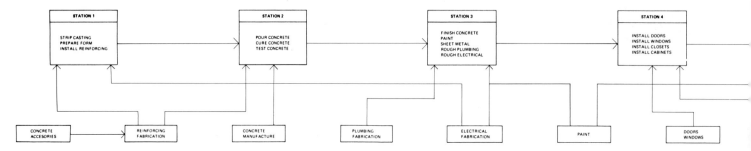

56. Puerto Rico Habitat assembly line.

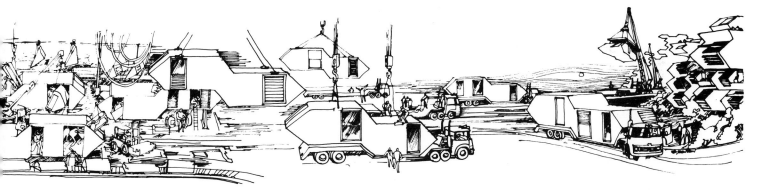

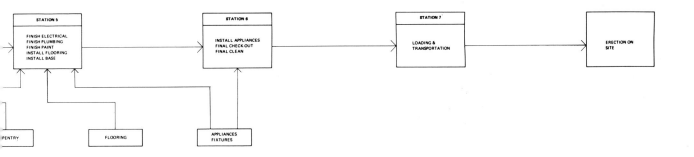

| STATION 5 | STATION 6 | STATION 7 | |
|---|---|---|---|
| FINISH ELECTRICAL<br>FINISH PLUMBING<br>FINISH PAINT<br>INSTALL FLOORING<br>INSTALL BASE | INSTALL APPLIANCES<br>FINAL CHECK-OUT<br>FINAL CLEAN | LOADING &<br>TRANSPORTATION | ERECTION ON<br>SITE |

CARPENTRY          FLOORING          APPLIANCES<br>FIXTURES

58. Construction of Puerto Rico Habitat. The jig for assembling the reinforcing steel cage.

59. The finished module transported in a plant by the travel lift.

60. The half-finished module is moved by the travel lift to the floor-casting station.

61. Foundation work on the site.

62. Finished boxes awaiting transportation to the site.

63. Detail of the kitchen.

**Erection Procedure**

1. Anchor Post-Tensioning Rods Into Coupler On Rods Below.
2. Set Module Above, Threading Rods Through Sleeves in Module Below.
3. Torque Rod Coupler Onto Rods.
4. Unhook Crane for Next Module.
5. Post-Tension Rod When Verical Stack is Complete.

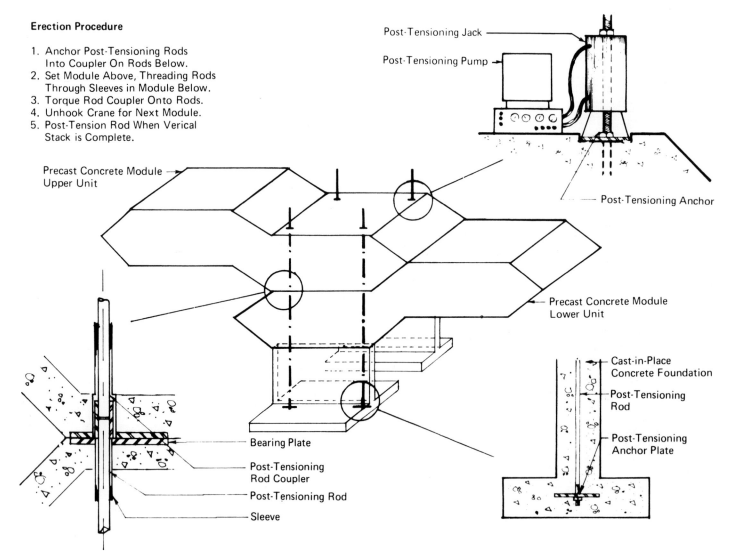

Post-Tensioning Jack

Post-Tensioning Pump

Post-Tensioning Anchor

Precast Concrete Module Upper Unit

Precast Concrete Module Lower Unit

Cast-in-Place Concrete Foundation

Post-Tensioning Rod

Post-Tensioning Anchor Plate

Bearing Plate

Post-Tensioning Rod Coupler

Post-Tensioning Rod

Sleeve

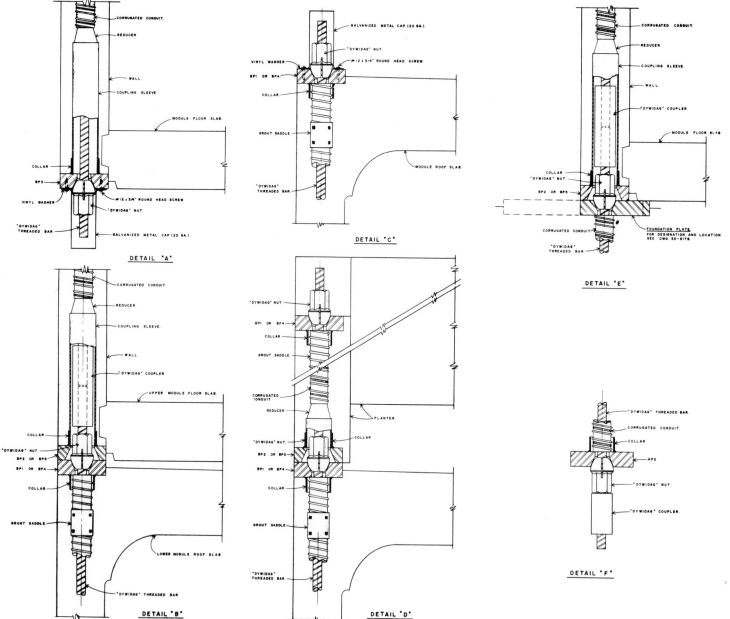

DETAIL "A"

DETAIL "B"

DETAIL "C"

DETAIL "D"

DETAIL "E"

DETAIL "F"

64-66. Post-tensioning details.

67. Reinforcing details at tip of module between the top casting and the floor casting.

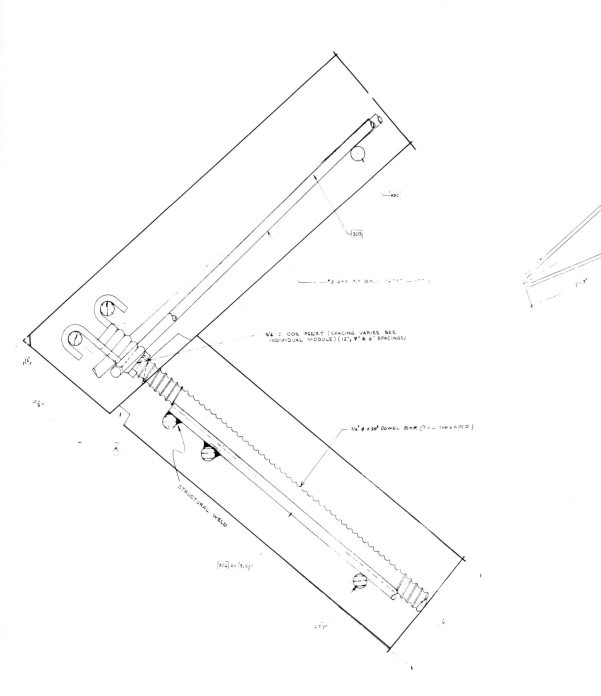

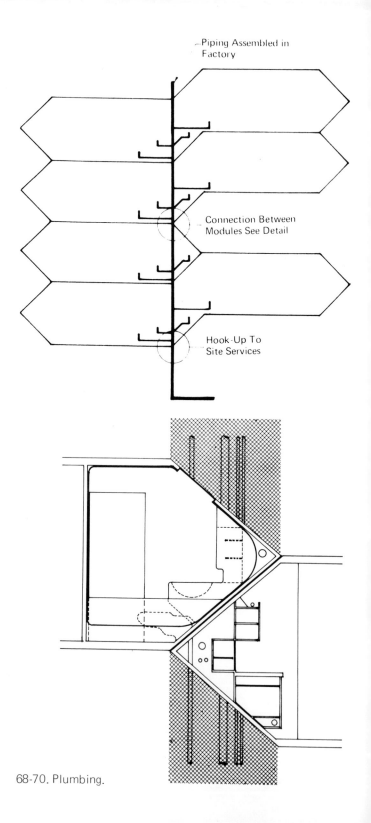

Piping Assembled in Factory

Connection Between Modules See Detail

Hook-Up To Site Services

68-70. Plumbing.

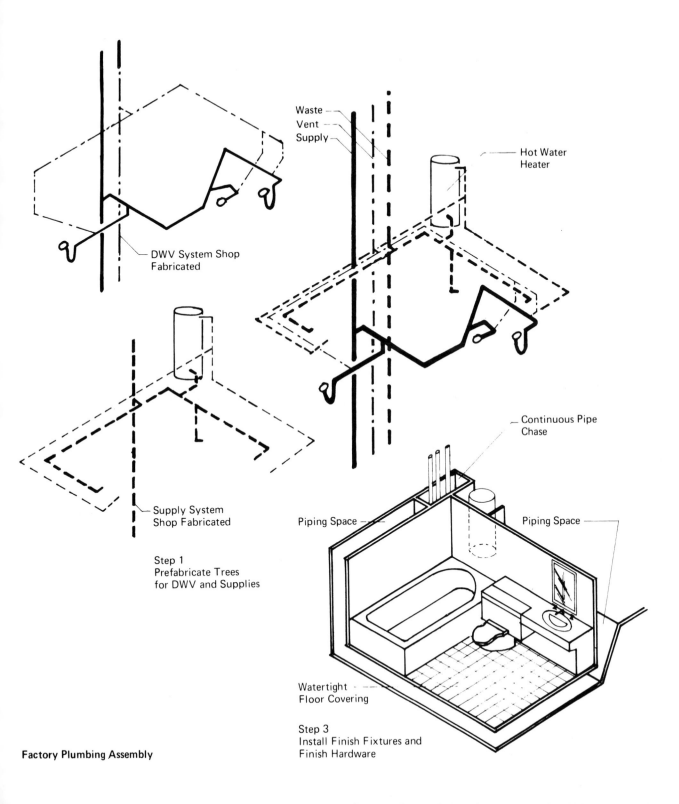

Waste
Vent
Supply

Hot Water
Heater

DWV System Shop
Fabricated

Supply System
Shop Fabricated

Step 1
Prefabricate Trees
for DWV and Supplies

Continuous Pipe
Chase

Piping Space

Piping Space

Watertight
Floor Covering

Step 3
Install Finish Fixtures and
Finish Hardware

**Factory Plumbing Assembly**

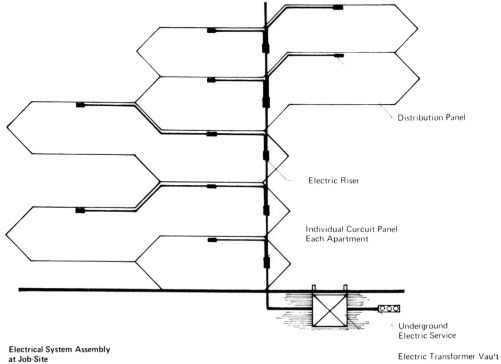

Distribution Panel

Electric Riser

Individual Curcuit Panel
Each Apartment

Underground
Electric Service

71, 72. Electric.

Electrical System Assembly
at Job-Site

Electric Transformer Vau't

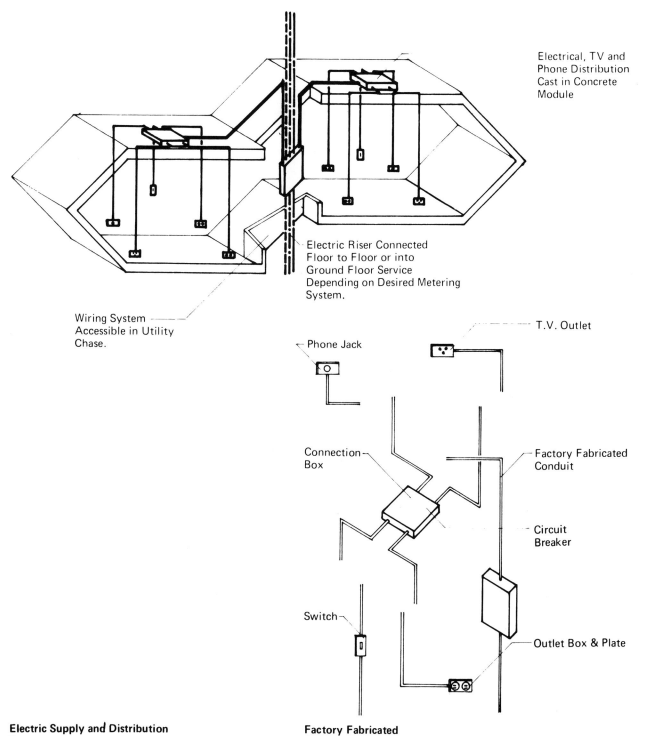

Electrical, TV and
Phone Distribution
Cast in Concrete
Module

Electric Riser Connected
Floor to Floor or into
Ground Floor Service
Depending on Desired Metering
System.

Wiring System
Accessible in Utility
Chase.

Phone Jack

T.V. Outlet

Connection
Box

Factory Fabricated
Conduit

Circuit
Breaker

Switch

Outlet Box & Plate

**Electric Supply and Distribution
System**

**Factory Fabricated
Components**

**Building in the Factory**
242-243
**Puerto Rico Habitat
Infrastructure,
Climate Control**

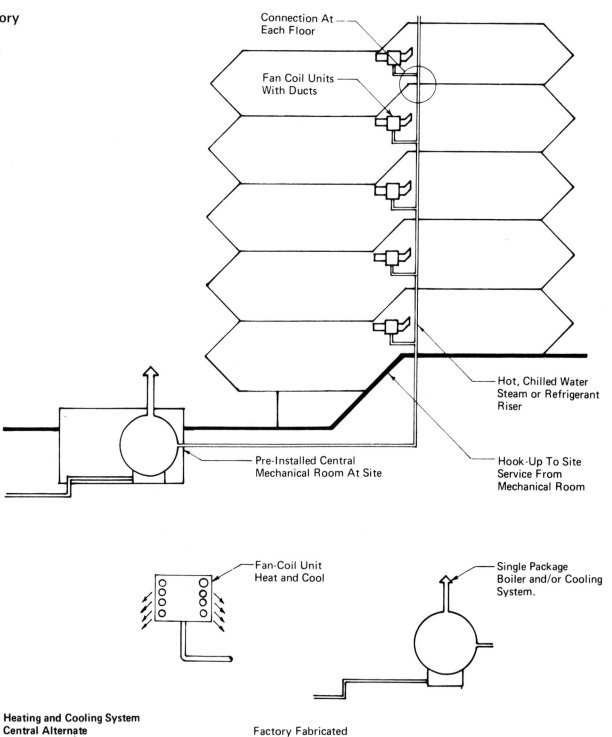

Connection At
Each Floor

Fan Coil Units
With Ducts

Hot, Chilled Water
Steam or Refrigerant
Riser

Pre-Installed Central
Mechanical Room At Site

Hook-Up To Site
Service From
Mechanical Room

Fan-Coil Unit
Heat and Cool

Single Package
Boiler and/or Cooling
System.

**Heating and Cooling System
Central Alternate
Gas or Oil Fuel**

Factory Fabricated
Components

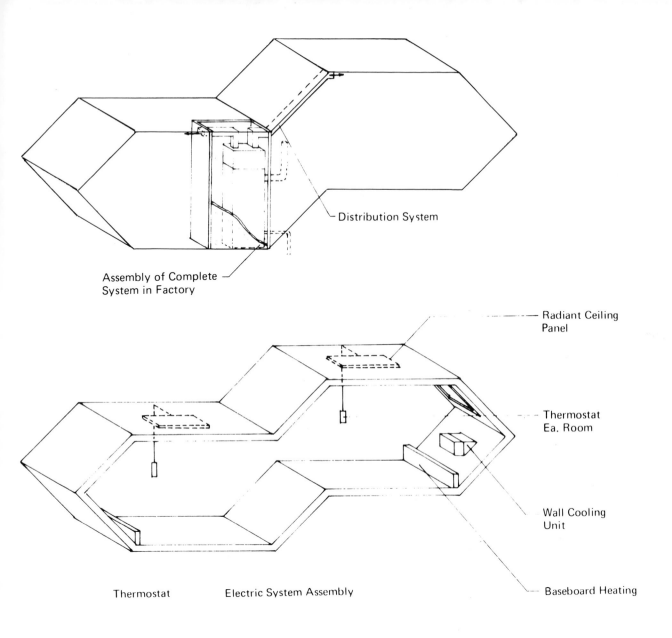

Distribution System

Assembly of Complete
System in Factory

Radiant Ceiling
Panel

Thermostat
Ea. Room

Wall Cooling
Unit

Baseboard Heating

Thermostat          Electric System Assembly

**Building in the Factory**
244-245
**Construction Alternatives
for Coldspring New Town:
Conventional Construction
versus Panels versus Boxes**

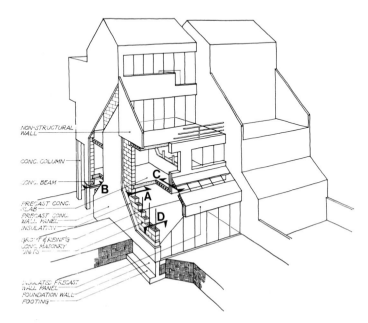

NON-STRUCTURAL
WALL

CONC. COLUMN

CONC. BEAM

PRECAST CONC.
SLAB
PRECAST CONC.
WALL PANEL
INSULATION

GROUT & REINF'G
CONC. MASONRY
UNITS

INSULATED PRECAST
WALL PANEL
FOUNDATION WALL
FOOTING

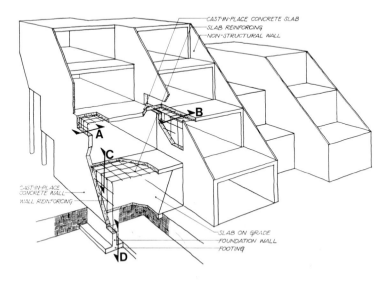

CAST-IN-PLACE CONCRETE SLAB
SLAB REINFORCING
NON-STRUCTURAL WALL

CAST-IN-PLACE
CONCRETE WALL
WALL REINFORCING

SLAB ON GRADE
FOUNDATION WALL
FOOTING

**Bricks versus panels versus boxes:**
The terms of the contract for Coldspring
New Town require that we should design
each housing type for three or four alternative construction systems, including conventional masonry construction, poured-in-place
concrete, semi-industrialized panel construction, and industrialized three-dimensional
modules. In the course of undertaking the
work we added another alternative of prefabricated factory-produced steel panels and
floor decks, thus investigating five alternate
systems.

The objective was to determine for a given
design what would be the optimum method
of construction. The interesting conclusion
of the study is that no particular system
came out with a resounding advantage over
the other.

Rather, the decision depended on the rate of
construction per year, local conditions re-
garding material and labor availability, and
the presence or lack of presence of a manufacturer in the area who was interested in
promoting a particular system. Thus, the
steel system was competitive at the time
when the steel industry was interested in
promoting the project.

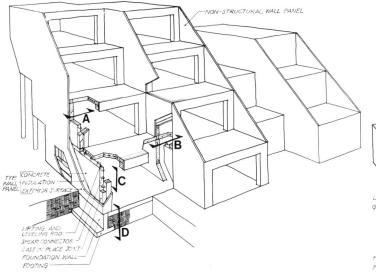

NON-STRUCTURAL WALL PANEL

A

B

TYP. CONCRETE
WALL INSULATION
PANEL EXTERIOR SURFACE

C

D

LIFTING AND
LEVELING ROD
SHEAR CONNECTOR
CAST-IN-PLACE JOINT
FOUNDATION WALL
FOOTING

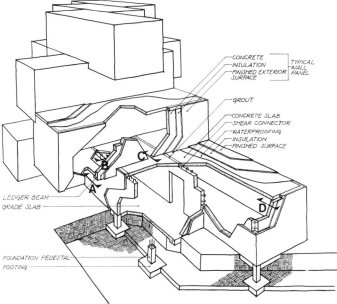

CONCRETE
INSULATION      TYPICAL
FINISHED EXTERIOR  WALL
SURFACE         PANEL

GROUT

CONCRETE SLAB
SHEAR CONNECTOR
WATERPROOFING
INSULATION
FINISHED SURFACE

A

B

C

D

LEDGER BEAM
GRADE SLAB

FOUNDATION PEDESTAL
FOOTING

Boxes were not an attractive alternative unless there was a manufacturer in the area who would put up a plant for other projects and unless the annual rate of construction was 700 units per year or over. Conventional construction was most competitive in the low-rise deck housing but least competitive in the high-rise or cluster housing.

75. Conventional masonry construction for deck housing.

76. Cast-in-place concrete cluster housing.

77. Cluster houses. Precast panel system.

78. Cluster housing. Crisscross panel systems. Prefabricated panels that are placed at right angles to one another.

**Building in the Factory**
246-247
**Construction Alternatives
for Coldspring New Town:
Conventional Construction
versus Panels versus Boxes**

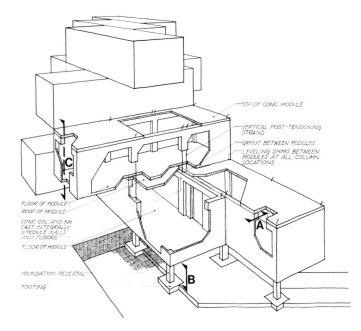

TOP OF CONC. MODULE
VERTICAL POST-TENSIONING STRAND
GROUT BETWEEN MODULES
LEVELING SHIMS BETWEEN MODULES AT ALL COLUMN LOCATIONS
FLOOR OF MODULE
ROOF OF MODULE
CONC. COL. AND BM. CAST INTEGRALLY W/MODULE WALLS AND FLOORS
FLOOR OF MODULE
FOUNDATION PEDESTAL
FOOTING

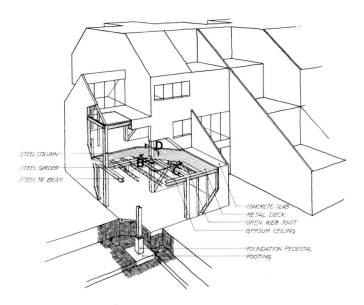

STEEL COLUMN
STEEL GIRDER
STEEL TIE BEAM
CONCRETE SLAB
METAL DECK
OPEN WEB JOIST
GYPSUM CEILING
FOUNDATION PEDESTAL
FOOTING

79. Cluster housing. Three-dimensional modular concrete boxes as the main construction element.

80. Cluster housing. Prefabricated steel truss panels and steel floor deck panels.

## FACTORY FEASIBILITY STUDY FOR ISRAEL HABITAT (1970)

Design Criteria Summary:

In summary, good plant layout has the following characteristics:

Planned materials flow pattern

Straight-line layout

Building constructed around a preplanned layout design

Straight, clear, marked aisles

Backtracking kept to minimum

Related operations close together

Production-time predictability

Minimum of scheduling difficulties

Minimum of goods-in-process

Easy adjustment to changing conditions

Plans for expansion

Maximum ratio of actual processing time to overall production time

Good quality with minimum inspection

Minimum materials-handling distances

Minimum of manual handling

No unnecessary rehandling of materials

Materials handled in unit loads

Minimum handling between operations

Materials efficiently removed from the work area

Materials handling being done by indirect labor

Orderly materials handling and storage

Good housekeeping

Busy employees, working at maximum efficiency

Design of Facilities and Equipment

With the objectives and design criteria previously developed, an Assembly Chart was diagramed for the Israel Habitat module as shown in Figure 81. The Assembly Chart separates the completed module into divisions of work that can be conveniently performed by similarly trained personnel and available equipment

**Building in the Factory**
248-249
**Third Generation Factory:**
**Planning a Factory for Israel**

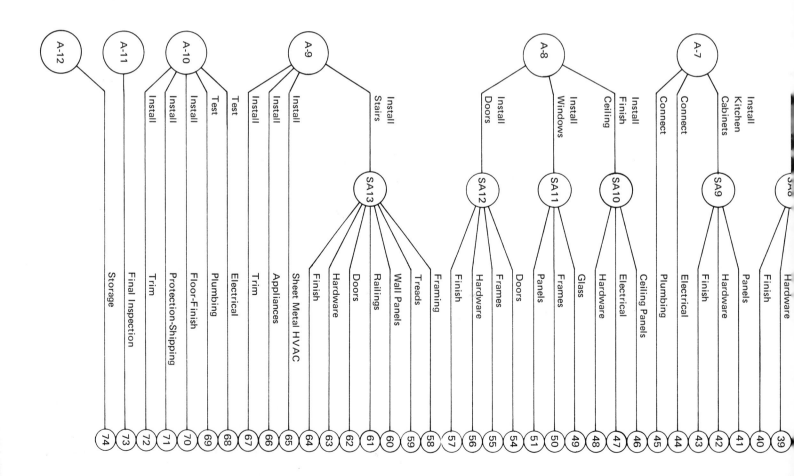

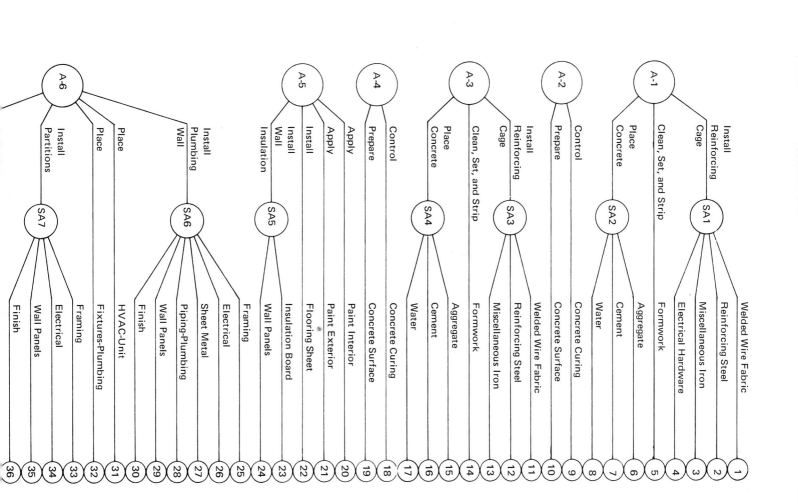

**Building in the Factory**
250-251
**Third Generation Factory:**
**Planning a Factory for Israel**

Legend:

 Materials-Handling Equipment for the Movement of Materials to and from Work Stations

 Assembly or Work Station

SA9 Subassembly or Prefinished Component

1,4,5 Storage of Raw Materials

Delay in the Handling of Materials

Materials-Handling Equipment:

M1  Truck and Trailer and/or Railroad

M2  Travel-lift

M3  Forklift

M4  Rail and Car

M5  Mixer Truck and/or Pump Placer

M6  Front-End Loader

M7  Conveyor, Belt, or Roller

M8  Trolley, Rail, and Hoist (Electric or Manual)

M9  Light Bridge Crane and Hoist

M10 Hand Truck

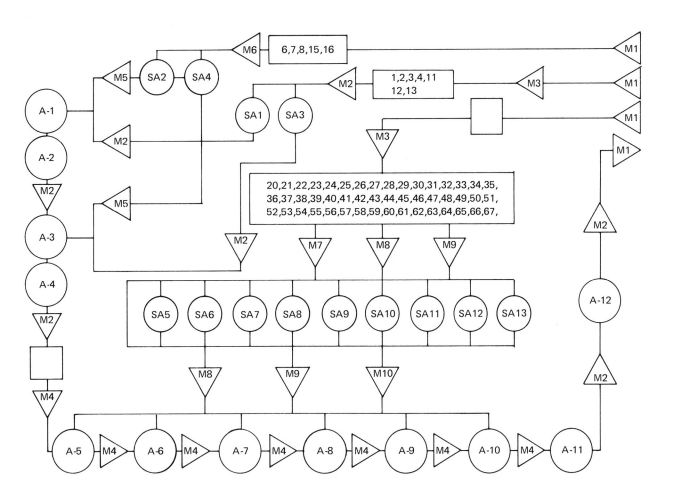

Building in the Factory
252-253
Third Generation Factory:
Planning a Factory for Israel

and tools. Raw materials are assembled into subassemblies that can be manufactured at a rate independent of the principle assembly line. The subassemblies may be purchased from an outside vendor, depending on the economic evaluation of the assembly.

The Assembly Chart has been developed on the basis that all work would be performed in the plant from basic raw materials. Not all modules will have the same assembly characteristics because some do not have bathrooms and kitchens. Production scheduling will group modules with similar characteristics.

The plant design was based on the assumption that the concrete module would be cast in two parts. The top part, or Cast A, would be cast at Station A-1. This casting would include the top slab and all exterior walls. After this casting gains approximately 3000 pounds per square inch, it is removed from the form and placed onto a second form to make the Cast B, or floor slab, at Station A-3. The curing cycle can vary depending on the design of the concrete mix. The recommended curing cycle for Chem-Stress Cement takes approximately 54 hours of controlled temperature and moisture. This cycle can be accommodated within the production flow at Stations A-1 through A-4. A production Flow Diagram was developed, as shown in Figure 83 from the Assembly Chart. Methods of handling the materials are indicated on the Flow Diagram and defined on the legend in Figure 82.

From the Assembly Chart and the Flow Diagram a suggested Plant Layout was developed, as shown in Figure 84. The plant layout would be the same for production capacities between 500 and 2000 units per year.

In general, the facilities and equipment for producing housing are standard and available in the U.S. market. The forms or molds, the curing system, and the system of moving the modules between assembly stations must be custom fabricated for the housing factory. Details for these systems are now shown in Figures 85, 86, and 87. Detailed specifications for the standard equipment required for the plant are found in the appendix (not included here). The forms,

84. Israel Habitat.
Plant Layout

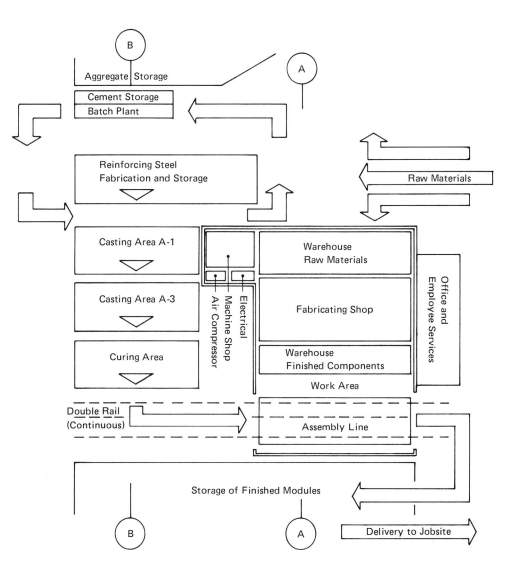

B

Aggregate Storage

Cement Storage

Batch Plant

A

Reinforcing Steel
Fabrication and Storage

Raw Materials

Casting Area A-1

Warehouse
Raw Materials

Air Compressor

Machine Shop

Electrical

Office and
Employee Services

Casting Area A-3

Fabricating Shop

Curing Area

Warehouse
Finished Components

Work Area

Double Rail
(Continuous)

Assembly Line

Storage of Finished Modules

B

A

Delivery to Jobsite

**Building in the Factory**
254-255
**Third Generation Factory:**
**Planning a Factory for Israel**

as shown in Figure 85, are designed to strip away completely from the casting before it is removed from the form. One of the major advantages of the use of Chem-Stress cement for casting the module is its characteristic to expand away from the inner mold as it cures. This will result in less production labor to strip the mold and a more refined casting because all joints in the form can be sealed and finished. The cost of the molds can be reduced by about 15 percent by eliminating the need to collapse the inside form.

The concrete curing system has been designed with the use of a portable kiln, as shown in Figure 86. This kiln is equipped with a hot air heater and an evaporator that will provide both the heat and the humidity required for the curing cycle. While this system is very economical for the smaller-capacity plants, it may be more economical to use radiant heat convectors charged from a hot oil boiler for the larger plants.

The assembly-line car and rail system, as shown in Figure 87, is used to carry the module from the curing stations to the various finishing stations. It can be propelled by either a forklift or a winch that can be activated in the desired cycle. The car can be fabricated from standard components, and the rail is standard light-gauge railroad rail. The rail should be mounted directly to the floor slab of the plant.

The equipment selected for the fabricating facility is based on the typical concrete module, as shown in Figure 88.

On the basis of two modules per housing unit, the required capacity of the concrete plant would be 88 cubic yards per day for a plant producing 500 units per year, 176 cubic yards per day for the plant producing 1000 units per year, and 352 cubic yards per day for a plant producing 2000 units per year. The maximum demand on the concrete plant could be as high as 44 cubic yards per hour. By assuming a concrete mix with approximately 8 sacks of cement per cubic yard of concrete, the demand for cement will be 176 barrels per day for the plant producing 500 units per year, 353 barrels per day for the plant pro-

85. Israel Habitat.
Schematic Mold Design-Cast A

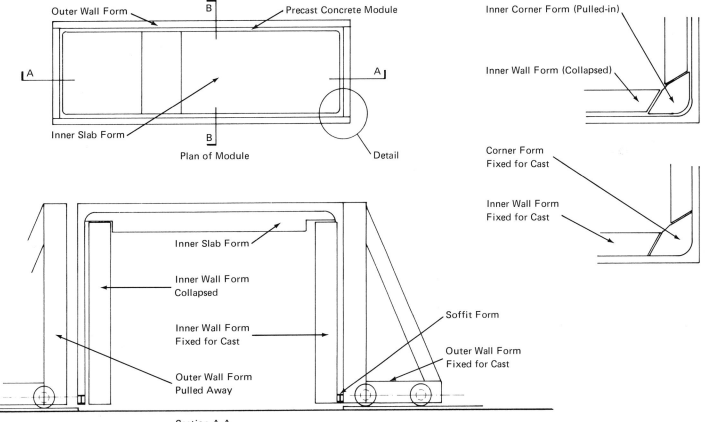

Outer Wall Form

B

Precast Concrete Module

A                                                    A

Inner Slab Form

B

Plan of Module

Detail

Inner Corner Form (Pulled-in)

Inner Wall Form (Collapsed)

Corner Form
Fixed for Cast

Inner Wall Form
Fixed for Cast

Inner Slab Form

Inner Wall Form
Collapsed

Inner Wall Form
Fixed for Cast

Outer Wall Form
Pulled Away

Soffit Form

Outer Wall Form
Fixed for Cast

Section A-A
Section B-B (Similar)

**Building in the Factory**
256-257
**Third Generation Factory:**
**Planning a Factory for Israel**

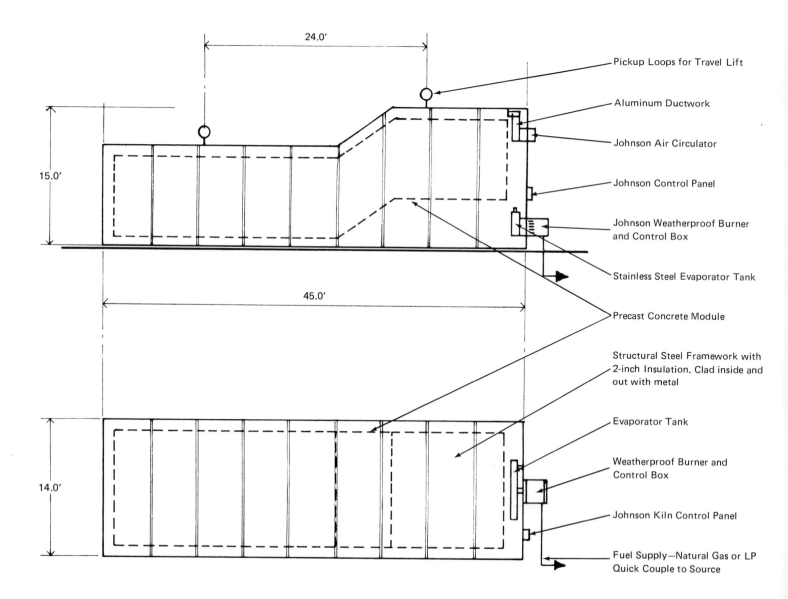

24.0'

15.0'

45.0'

14.0'

Pickup Loops for Travel Lift

Aluminum Ductwork

Johnson Air Circulator

Johnson Control Panel

Johnson Weatherproof Burner
and Control Box

Stainless Steel Evaporator Tank

Precast Concrete Module

Structural Steel Framework with
2-inch Insulation. Clad inside and
out with metal

Evaporator Tank

Weatherproof Burner and
Control Box

Johnson Kiln Control Panel

Fuel Supply—Natural Gas or LP
Quick Couple to Source

86. Israel Habitat.
Kiln Concrete Curing System

87. Israel Habitat.
Assembly Line Rail and Car

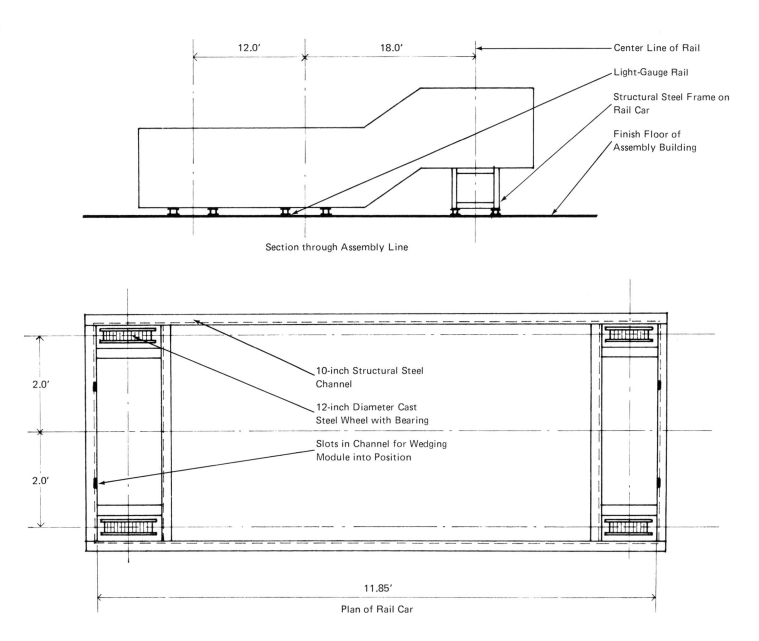

12.0'   18.0'

Center Line of Rail

Light-Gauge Rail

Structural Steel Frame on
Rail Car

Finish Floor of
Assembly Building

Section through Assembly Line

2.0'

2.0'

10-inch Structural Steel
Channel

12-inch Diameter Cast
Steel Wheel with Bearing

Slots in Channel for Wedging
Module into Position

11.85'

Plan of Rail Car

**Building in the Factory**
258-259
**Third Generation Factory:
Planning a Factory for Israel**

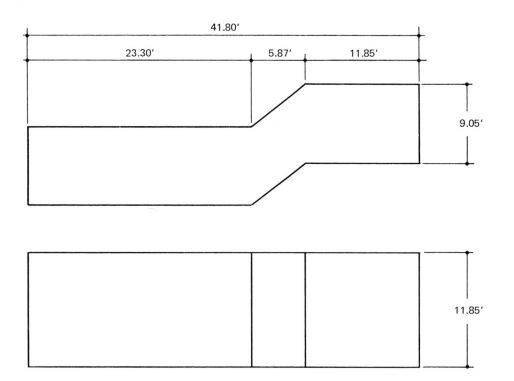

| | Surface Area | Volume | Weight |
|---|---|---|---|
| | square feet | cubic yards | pounds |
| Top Slab | 505 | 6.14 | 24,900 |
| Side (1) | 344 | 3.75 | 15,210 |
| Side (2) | 344 | 3.75 | 15,210 |
| End (1) | 94 | 1.03 | 4,180 |
| End (2) | 94 | 1.03 | 4,180 |
| Total | 1381 | 15.71 | 63,680 |
| Bottom Slab | 505 | 6.14 | 24,900 |
| Total | 1886 | 21.84 | 88,580 |

88. Israel Habitat.
Physical Properties
Typical Module

ducing 1000 units per year, and 704 barrels per day for the plant producing 2000 units per year.

An estimate of the cost of the facilities and equipment is made for plants having the production capacity of 500, 1000, and 2000 housing units per year. The equipment specifications are based on proved methods and practices that minimize the utilization of labor. There is considerable latitude in modifying the degree of mechanization and materials-handling equipment specified, based on local labor conditions and the availability of prefabricated subassemblies. Particular consideration was made in selecting equipment that was portable and minimized fixed installation facilities. It should be noted that the cost estimates are based on U.S. prices, F.O.B. New York, without taxes, duty, or shipping charges. It is estimated that a fabricating plant, complete with concrete plant, enclosed warehouse and assembly line, and hauling and erection equipment will be $1,306,393, $1,712,392, and $3,024,843 for plants with production capacities of 500, 1000, and 2000 dwelling units per year, respectively.

Conclusions and Recommendations

From an analysis of the fixed costs it can be concluded that the greater productive plant (2000 units per year) is more economical to operate than the smaller plants. This is the result of being able to amortize the fixed cost over a greater number of units.

The general and administrative personnel required to operate the larger plant is not proportional to the amount of personnel required to operate the smaller plant. Once the framework of the housing organization is established, it can be expanded to handle efficiently a production capacity. There is a limit to the minimum size of the organization that can effectively operate a plant. To staff an organization less than that for the 500 units per year plant would result in a sacrifice in production efficiency.

The indirect labor cost remains fixed through the various production levels because production capacity is expanded by the addition of direct labor and

**Building in the Factory**
260-261
**Third Generation Factory:
Planning a Factory for Israel**

equipment. A casting superintendent can efficiently supervise six foremen as well as two foremen.

The two major items that influence the plant amortization cost are the casting forms and the hauling and erection equipment. The amortization is the same for both the 1000-unit plant and the 2000-unit plant. The form amortization for each plant is the same because they control the production capacity. If four modules are to be completed each day, then four castings must be produced each day. The hauling and erection equipment amortization is the same for the 1000- and 2000-unit plants because the equipment is operating at capacity for these conditions. It was estimated that each crane could set eight modules, or four dwelling units each day. This is an average, including setup and moving time. It should be noted that a crane operated at only 50 percent of capacity, as shown for the 500-unit plant, doubles the amortization charges against each housing unit produced. The evaluation of cost savings as a result of a higher production rate should be based on whether the plant and equipment are operating at full capacity. It should be noted that a 2000-unit per year plant operating at 60 percent of rated capacity would generate the same fixed charges as a 500-unit plant operating at 100 percent of capacity. It is recommended that the design criteria be established to assure near peak capacity operation. The plant should be designed for expansion to meet the market growth. This study indicates only the magnitude of fixed operating cost for plants operating at 100 percent of design capacity. If the value of the completed housing unit is assumed to be equivalent to $10,000, the difference in fixed operating cost is only 4 percent between the 500-unit plant and the 2000-unit plant.

The possibility of moving the factory facilities and equipment was evaluated. Relocation of the facility could be a possible solution to overcome high transportation cost or legal and safety limits on the use of the highway system. If the analysis is made on the basis of economics, the cost of moving the facility can be compared to the cost of transportation. The feasibility will depend entirely on the quantity of production over which the relocation cost can be amortized. Each situation must be evaluated individually. However, it can be concluded that the relocation of the production facilities is completely feasible. For a project of 2000 units, the increase in cost of a $10,000 dwelling unit would be only 2.5 percent.

Meeting Places
262-263
Program for San Francisco
State College
Written by Member of
Committee

| WE NEED PLACES FOR ..... | ONE PERSON | A COUPLE OF PEOPLE | A FEW PEOPLE | QUITE A FEW PEOPLE | A LOT OF PEOPLE | EVERYBODY |
|---|---|---|---|---|---|---|
| talking/listening/thinking/communing/ plotting/convincing/sharing/starting/ ending things without interruption from others - from their passage, their noise or their activities, and from mechanical or climatic factors | | little places | little spaces / spaces inside | big spaces inside | outside space | Washington Square |
| looking at things without interruption for instance... | TV | books | paintings/prints/photographs / sculpture | ballet / light shows / films | demonstrations / clouds/trees/sky | parades / horseracing |
| listening to and looking at things | | records/tapes / ourselves think / harmonicas / telephones | folk singers / poetry readings | chamber music / concerts / operas | somebody talk / films / big concerts / mass meetings / demonstrations | Beatles |
| doing things that we can't do by ourselves or that we don't have the facilities to do at home | | darkrooms / workshops | dancing together / making multiple images / making films and TV tapes | making music / making many copies | marching / singing out loud | mass meetings |
| leaving personal things where they're safe | | checkroom / lockers / lockable spaces | file cabinets | cabinets/big lockers / safes/"museums"/storage rooms | suites of space | |
| leaving things for somebody else to respond to | | message centers / bulletin boards | collections / one-man shows | group shows / libraries | sign-up places / signboards | the whole environment |
| eating things that we bring with us/ eating things that we buy and eat there/eating things that somebody else brings to us - waitresses | | niches/sitting places / outdoor places with blackbirds | indoor places / little corners | small spaces / larger spaces | big spaces | Piazza San Marco |
| giving people things | | | physical relief places - rest rooms / sitting places/resting places/information about things / napping places | showers | looking out of places / sitting together places / a sense of beauty / a sense of well being | |
| buying things | | stamps | original prints/paintings/jewelry | tickets to things / books and magazines / banking | newspapers / services - laundry / cleaners | |
| preparing things for future use, or sending away things that have been used/ or storing things between uses | | checkrooms / garbage cans | kitchens / gallery shipping / maintainence/janitorial supplies | practice and rehearsal rooms | stockrooms / scene shops | gallery storage / service facilities |

Ralph Putzker

# 4

MEETING PLACES

Program

When we began working on the San Francisco State College Student Union Building, we were handed a program that had been written two years earlier. It was the kind of conventional program one usually gets from a client. It had a detailed discussion of quantitative space requirements: the number of meetings held weekly and daily by various student organizations, the number of people who frequented the cafeteria every day, and so forth.

I explained that this kind of quantitative program was not a point of departure into the design; that I thought the program had to be expanded to include a sense of the qualitative requirements for the various spaces. The preparation of a qualitative program was where architect and client could really interact and clarify objectives. A separate contract was issued to cover this work.

Making a quantitative program is fairly straightforward, and before long, we had either confirmed or modified the numbers in the original program. For instance, they had stated that fourteen hundred people had to be fed at one time during lunch. It isn't difficult to calculate what that means in terms of floor area. But the students said a cafeteria-style feeding factory was not the type of environment and eating experience they wanted. So we talked about what they did want. They pointed to Telegraph Street in Berkeley, where there are about thirty different small restaurants, all of them fairly reasonably priced, each selling its own specialized food: hamburger joints, Chinese food, a Mexican restaurant. Each supplied food that was no more expensive than the SFS College cafeteria. So the idea was born that instead of having one giant kitchen and one great dining hall we could have a central storage and preparation kitchen that would supply ingredients to half a dozen specialized kitchens, operating independently, each selling different food and serving it in a particular small space. So that we had a Chinese restaurant, a hot dog place, a cheese and wine place, and a health food place, all inside the Union building.

Another example of a qualitative program parameter concerned the meeting rooms that were needed. The students' projected statistics showed that on certain days they would need seven rooms accommodating thirty people each; on other days they'd need two rooms for two hundred people and several rooms for fifteen or thirty. Once in a while they would want to hold student society meetings that usually attract about a thousand students. If we had simply added up the number of meeting rooms involved, they would have required three times the amount of space that the budget for the total building would have been able to provide. We came to the conclusion that what they needed was a rearrangeable set of spaces that could be opened up to hold one thousand or broken down into ten small rooms for twenty or any other combination.

But we didn't want the rooms to feel like an impersonal subdivided piece of space the way most meeting rooms in hotels and convention centers do. We wanted subdivisible space that would maintain its spatial and geometric integrity, whatever its configuration.

Similar discussions took place about the nature of a meeting hall itself. A room accommodating thirty people might be used for discussions in the round, or a lecture, a film, or a modern dance session. The sort of room that suited these activities might have a flat, stepped, or dished floor, brilliant light, subdued light, or no light at all.

We replied with a series of "form diagrams," suggesting rooms that, for example, could be rearranged from a flat floor to a bowl-shaped floor or to one sloped in a single direction. Through these diagrams we were able to capture the intent of requirements that can be evoked only by saying that a place should be flooded with sunlight and filled with plants, or that a recreational pool have islands to lounge on or cascading waterfalls to sit beneath.

The form diagrams gave some broad organizational guidelines. We knew we wanted people to walk right through the building, so it had somehow to arch over the major campus walkways. We knew we wanted each room to grow higher as it grew wider, and to receive natural light in proportion to its size and depth.

We could have said that, for each different type of space, we should use the type of structural system best suited to it; say, long span, open web joists for the theater, or concrete flat slabs for the offices. Perhaps in simple terms of economy and efficiency, this would have been right. But in terms of quality, I don't think it would have been right. When you choose the system you build with, to a large extent you determine the quality of space. The office buildings and apartment houses that have been built in the last fifty years are all built with the same system: an orthogonal frame, a flat slab, and exterior wall with windows. The quality of space and light is the same in all of them. Everyone can predict how they will be furnished, what kind of partitions and subcomponents will be used. No matter how imaginative the designer or decorator is who chooses the interior colors, textures, and furnishings, what we experience is basically the same. The floor and ceiling are always parallel and of constant height; natural light comes only through a horizontal band of windows at the side.

During the design of the San Francisco Student Union project, we spent several months in the office trying to put together a building system that would, by its very nature, give us the environmental qualities we wanted.

In the course of one of the meetings with the students, I joked with them that if I brought a pile of the bent cardboard pieces from the office, they could put together the building for themselves. But then I realized that that was more than a joke. If the students at San Francisco State had taken those cardboard bents and grouped and combined them in a different arrangement from the one I suggested, and if they followed the rules of combination, the most basic qualities of the building would have remained intact. Spaces would have grown proportionately higher as they grew larger in area; light would still enter the building in the same way; you could still have walked up and over the building from the surrounding park and entered the structure at many levels; plant life and structure would still interpenetrate; in short, it would be the same environment. A structure formed by this kind of a generating system could be likened to a fugue. You design you basic theme, or chord, and determine the rules by which it can be combined. The form, whether it is musical or physical, is the result of those rules of permutation.

Perhaps there is a certain laziness in my own personal preference for this method of design. It takes a lot of work to "compose" a building in the conventional way, with elevations and perspective sketches. I might do it well or badly, I'm not sure. But my "formula," let me call it, does a lot of things for me. In Habitat, I worked out a spiral system for putting modules in clusters at 45 degrees to the pedestrian streets. Then I elaborated that generalized system and com-

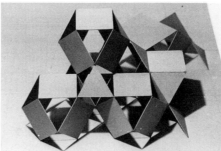
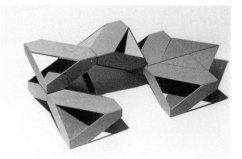

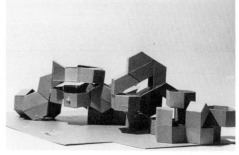

2-7. The evolution of the San Francisco State Union building system. The phoneticization of volumes and their juxtaposition in the total building mass.
  A series of alternative studies of the structural system, circulation pattern, and space-enclosing geometry.

bined clusters to adapt to the site. And presto—you have your environment, you go through big spaces, then small spaces, and protrusions and recessions, concave and convex, and you just about get dizzy having all these things happening. And I didn't have to work at it at all. It just all happened, generated by the system. Paul Rudolph's buildings have rich spaces. But it seems to me that he has to labor over every space; a balcony penetrating here, a window there. He's very good at it, but he has good mornings and bad mornings; his buildings are dependent on a compositional skill. I feel that my method is less arbitrary. Once I know that if the basic system is not forced, that it has been generated by and can therefore accommodate both the qualitative and functional requirements of the building, I can get enormous richness and variety of spaces, without ever drawing elevations. No elevations were drawn of Habitat 67 or Puerto Rico Habitat, or the San Francisco Union. There was simply a matrix, plotted with the code numbers of the various components. The structures are too complex three-dimensionally to be represented any other way.

People often ask me, "When are you going to market a Habitat toy?" They look at Habitat and say, "Oh yeah, I did that with my blocks when I was a kid." This association with toys comes up all the time, and it seems accurately to describe the quality of the environments I've designed. I don't find it good or bad. I just find it important that people respond with a sense of whimsy, and that they feel that they might be able to manipulate it themselves. They don't feel mystified by it.

I've tried to discover all the components that make a good toy, with a set of rules for the game that will make it adaptable to different places and scales of development. And then, if they wish, people can make formal compositions with the elements, as they do with vernacular techniques such as the adobe wall and dome. People can put them together any way they choose, without disrupting the unity of a village. The elements, the common denominators, are not determined by some desire for a particular "style."

When Philip Johnson was the master plan architect for Welfare Island in New York, he thought that by specifying what type of window and walls could be used it would assure some kind of unity and sense of order throughout the development, although the buildings were to be designed by different architects. He picked a stylistic detail, hoping that that would tie it all together. This must have seemed sound reasoning because we can all point to successful precedents for it in the Georgian period of English architecture. The Georgians had a certain vocabulary of the way windows were made, and how a portico and a set of steps were used at an entrance, that gave a certain measure of unity and continuity to the neighborhood. But I think that there is a deeper structure to that unity. It isn't simply the detailing of the masonry. For example, behind the Georgian facade there was the whole concept of the urban town house, the tall, narrow house that shared its sidewalls with its neighbors, and the crescent, or square, or oval public space that all the houses formed together. A common denominator like a square window in a brick wall, in an age when we have such a vast choice of materials, is too superficial either to be respected by the other architects or to achieve a unified whole.

Continuity has to do with the scale of the openings and components of a structure, but it has also to do with the way the building occupies the land and the way it relates to the existing pattern of movement through the city, the system of grouping dwellings in relation to orientation, view, circulation, the expression of the scale of dwelling and cluster and the hierarchy of private and public open spaces.

Instead of just picking a window detail, Johnson could have said that each house should have a garden, or every unit should face south, or every unit should have a view of the Manhattan skyline, or all units should be entered from a pedestrian circulation system that is open to the air and has the qualities of a public street. Then there would have been more substance to the common denominator.

Whenever architects talk about urban meeting places, it seems that they find themselves referring to Italian piazzas or French boulevards of past centuries. No one seems very entranced with anything built more recently, nor do we seem capable of reproducing the success of these older places. Perhaps one way of talking about those plazas or meeting places in a contemporary way is to look at the modern shopping center. It has some of the ingredients that a real meeting place needs but is lacking in many others.

Take Montreal's Place Ville Marie, for example. It is an underground maze of shops and corridors, through which people constantly move because there is a railway station, a subway station, and a large hotel at one end of it and the work destination of many at the other. Approximately fifty thousand people work in the skyscrapers above. Over the indoor shopping area is a huge flat plaza, which is used in the summer (three months in Montreal) and which is desolate the rest of the year. As a public place, a meeting place, the failure of Place Ville Marie is that there is never any opportunity to comprehend the total; the indoor and the outdoor are brutally separated; one cannot sit and enjoy the spectacle of all the other people around. It is essentially a place made up of long corridors that have practically no natural light. In short, the physical structure of the center does not facilitate the flowering of a diversified and intense urban life as we associate it with great meeting places.

Montreal has other new meeting places. Two adjacent Montreal shopping centers, Westmount Square and Alexis Nihon Plaza, which is the most successful meeting place the city has built. It is always full of life. People meet there; people hang around there. Basically it too is just a shopping center, but the last station of the subway line is beneath it, and all the connecting buses are outside. It has a large glass-roofed space, three stories high, which lets you comprehend the whole space and, at once, all that is going on in it.

Recently, I went to Columbia, Maryland, and one of the first things I was taken to see was the shopping center. It was, by any standard, a very exciting place. It was filled with people, and the space-framed glass roof created a really pleasant quality of light. But, from the outside, all you can see are blank walls, with a couple of slots to sneak through. Around that are parking decks and parking lots. Five hundred feet away there is a lake. Next to it, there are two office buildings, and next to them, an exhibit building. Two thousand feet in the other direction is a music bowl. Where is the town center? Is the library part of the town center? If so, why does the average person feel he ought to get into his car and drive to it from the shopping center? Because it is on the other side of a parkway and there is no connection conducive to walking. The mall should have been the town center. The lake should have come into the mall. The library should have opened off it and some of the housing could have hovered over it. The music center could have been connected to it too. Entry to the mall should have been obvious, its links with the rest of the residential area, both physical and visual, should have been clear. It should never have been surrounded by a sea of cars and parking structures. The cars could have been under or over it. Now there is a barrier between the center and the rest of the town. The park spaces could have joined it in such a way that you could do your errands in the marketplace, go for a stroll outside, and then come back again. It would have not cost one more cent to do that. The shortcomings of the Columbia Plan are not based in economics but in the misunderstanding of the ingredients of urban life.

During the preliminary discussions for the Coldspring New Town in Baltimore, which were attended by James Rouse who built Columbia and is also the developer for Coldspring, I was asked by a journalist, "In what way do you feel Coldspring will differ from Columbia?" I told him that in Columbia the land was cut up into parcels divided by roads. Within the parcels you had various structures: some housing, some shopping areas, some schools. And the way you get from one place to another is by getting in your car and driving along the roads. Of course, in some cases you could walk along the edge of the road on the sidewalk, but it is totally subordinated in scale to the movement of the car; it is unsheltered and, therefore, not really conducive to pedestrian movement. But, in Coldspring, the buildings are the major organizers of movement, and the road moves through them or under them, and the pedestrian is sheltered within them. All the facilities—the housing, the shopping, the hotel, the cinema, the church, the schools—are part of an integrated structure, and the open space is a continuous system too, rather than just a collection of "aprons" related to individual structures. It is a fundamentally different pattern of development.

**San Francisco State College Student Union**
The location of the college union within the
campus generated the building's organization; it was to be located at the crossroads
of all paths of pedestrian movement on campus. The building could have become a barrier, an object to be reluctantly avoided by
walking around it or, alternatively, could
become a major interchange. Rather than
divert pedestrian circulation around it, the
massing and the organization of the building
attempts to capture this movement and
direct it through the archlike structure.

The existing buildings around the campus
green are primarily painted boxlike concrete
frame structures, forming a hard edge to its
pine-studded lawn. I attempted to integrate
the Union with the campus green and not
the surrounding structures. By extending up
over the structure, making the building glass
and grass, it would have been possible for
students to climb on and sit on the battered
walls of the building, and for the park and
structure to become one.

Varied facilities serving thousands of people
were to be grouped within a single structure.
At midday in a period of fifteen minutes, as
many as five thousand students might arrive
or depart. Conventional doors and lobbies,
central stairs, and elevators alone would not
have accommodated this with comfort. So
in addition, the whole exterior of the building itself become a second system of movement, a continuous network of stairs and
landings and entrances ascending on the inclined surface of the structure.

The program for the union included office
and work space; commercial space for selling
books and crafts and clothes; dining halls,
small meeting rooms, and large assembly
halls. It is generally assumed that such a
building does not lend itself to any form of
standardized modular organization. In this
project we attempted, however, to develop a
method of construction in which a small
number of repetitive elements that could be
mass-produced and easily assembled on the
site would be grouped in a variety of ways
to form a hierarchy of spaces from the smallest to the largest required. We chose a single
repetitive module with auxiliary floor slab
elements, which could be grouped to form
rooms and spaces of varied size and volume,
quality of light, height, and span without
sacrificing the basic requirement of repetition for easy and fast construction and
economy.

The basic bent shape modular element was
to be an open "U," spanning 30 feet with
its vertical legs inclined to 45 degrees. The
unit was to be precast in concrete 4 inches
thick with edge beams 8 inches thick; the
floor slabs were to be precast in octagonal
sections. There were also auxiliary precast
pieces to complete the enclosure of the
spaces. Upon completion of each floor, 3
inches of concrete topping was to be poured
over the slab to achieve structural continuity.

In the large rooms, such as the assembly hall, the bents (transverse frameworks) are grouped on top of one another, forming a domelike space with a span of 70 feet by 100 feet. In the office section, where many small rooms were required, the bent is used on its side as a vertical wall, eliminating the problem of loss of headroom that results when the bent is in its normal position. The modular bent can provide sloping floors as well, for the meeting rooms and theater.

The distribution of mechanical services was provided by vertical shafts and a horizontal space enclosed by a suspended ceiling. Ideally, we would have liked to incorporate all this in the bent panel, but the complexity of the problem of joints and connections was too great to be solved in a project of limited scale.

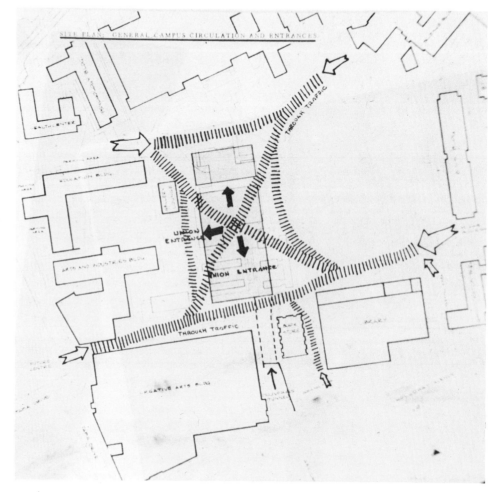

9. The union is designed to accommodate the crossing of major campus pedestrian circulation paths.

10. The campus green at midday.

11. Roof plan of the union showing its position on the campus green.

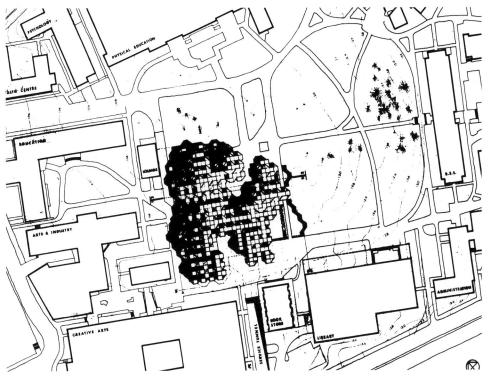

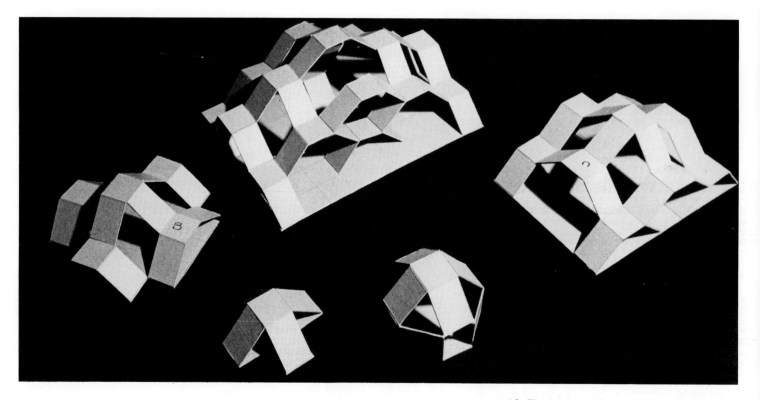

12. The basic system as finally evolved: a repetitive structural bent capable of forming rooms ranging in size from 20 to 100 feet in span and from one story to four stories in volume.

13, 14. The system generates a circulation system of "walking up the walls" and the basket-weave roof pattern generates vertical spaces for the introduction of mechanical shafts.

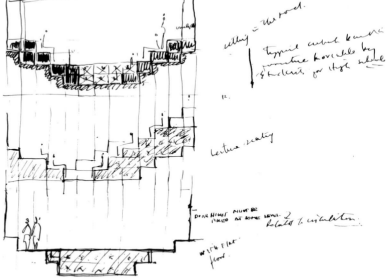

16. Floor plan, level 3.

17. Floor plan, level 6.

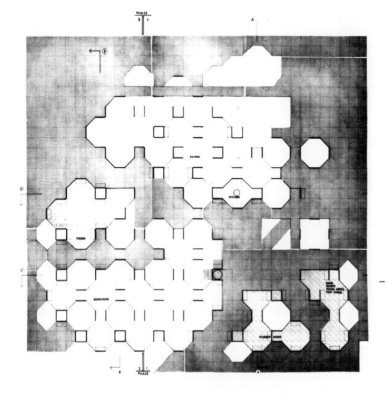

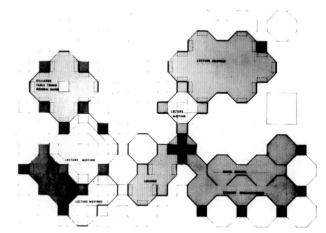

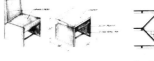

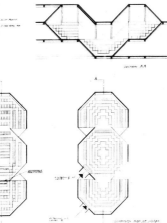

18. Special seats can change the contours of the room.

19. Hinged panels convert several small meeting rooms into a large hall.

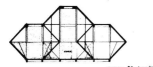

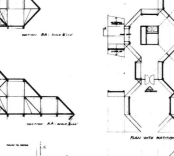

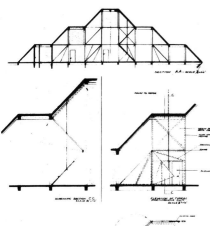

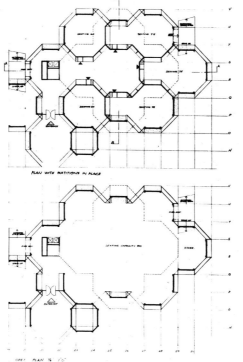

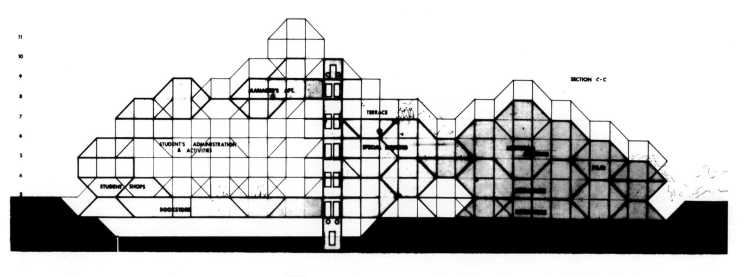

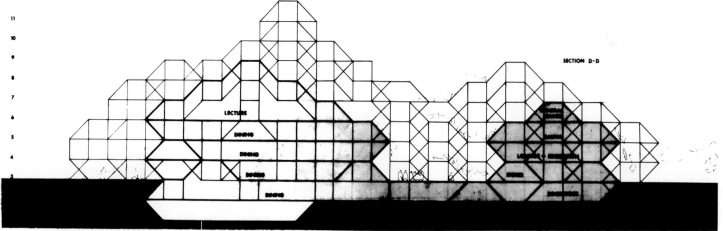

32. General view of the union from the west, showing the campus path penetrating through the building.

**Meeting Places**
284-285
**San Francisco State College**
**Student Union**
**Utilization of Inclined Walls**

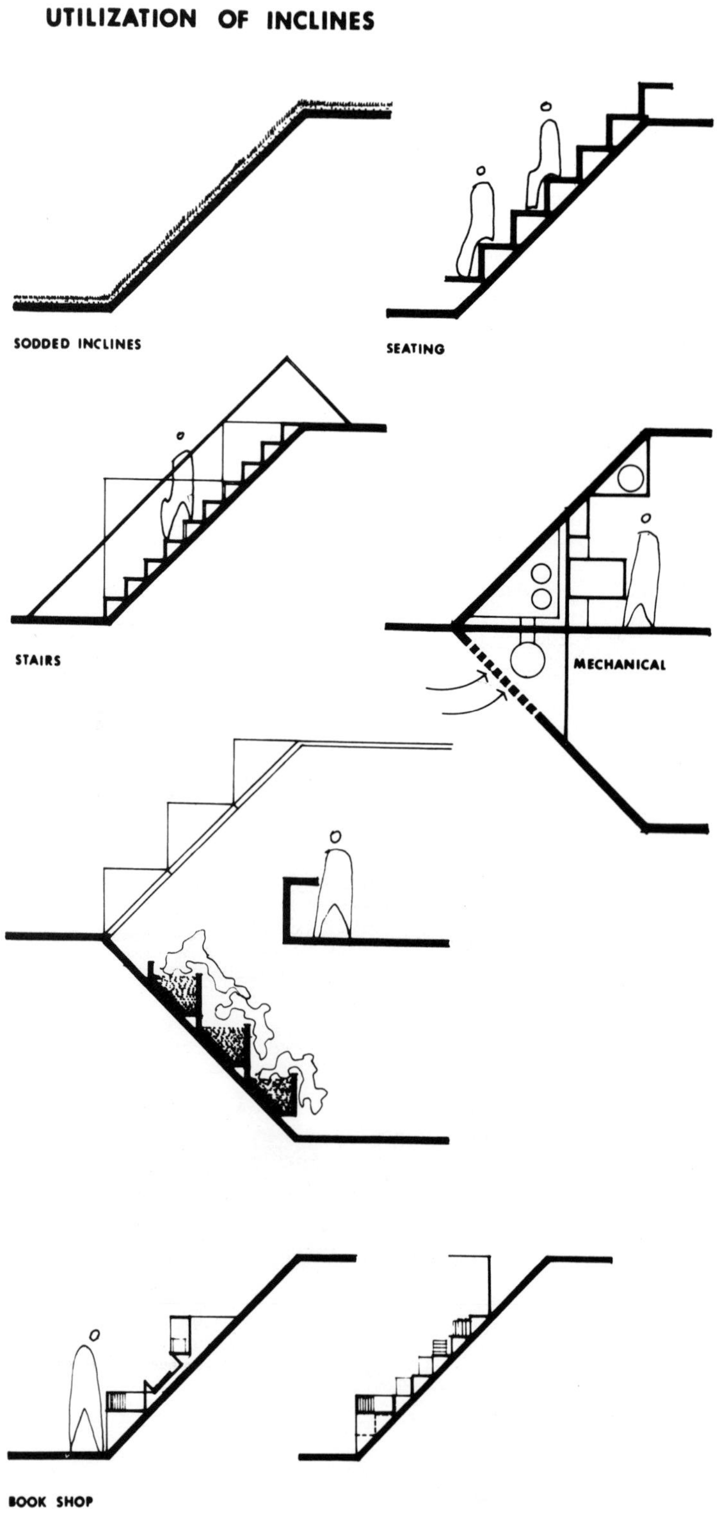

UTILIZATION OF INCLINES

SODDED INCLINES

SEATING

STAIRS

MECHANICAL

BOOK SHOP

34. Diagram explaining the utilization of the spaces formed by the inclined walls. A. Planting on incline. B. Stairs on incline. C. Exterior seating on the inclined wall. D. Mechanical spaces and built-in furniture. E. Interior garden. F. Bookstore display.

35. San Francisco State College: exterior view of terraces, outdoor stairs, and the dining room.

36. View of the interior of the dining room.

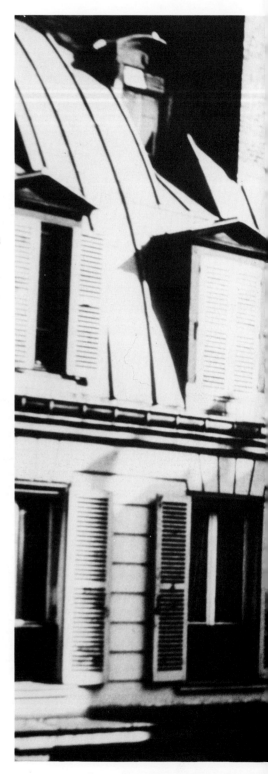

**Centre du Plateau Beaubourg,
Competition Entry (1971)**

The program for the competition envisioned this "cultural center" as an urban meeting place with a national library, museums, theaters, restaurants, and cafés. It seemed to me that it was essential for the organization of the total complex to be understood at the moment of arrival. The problem was to give a sense of place that would be more than library and museum. The building forms a deep hexagonal dish, excavated six stories below street level, and an octahedral space frame arching over it. The configuration of the frame is something like two trapezoidal planes inclined in opposite directions and locked together at their point of intersection. The structure system allowed great versatility in subdividing and changing spaces.

From two opposing corners of the site the visitor sees only terraces of glass and greenery that can be scaled by many staircases; from the other two corners the whole of the sheltered superspace is visible. The real enclosing walls of the complex are the facades of the surrounding older Paris buildings.

The northern inclined structure accommodates the museum; the southern, the library and a rooftop restaurant. At street level and at the various Métro levels, there are additional galleries and halls. The entire roof becomes a terraced park.

The dishlike space is sheltered by the space frame structure like a tree, with light and sun penetrating the membrane of library and museum to the glazed galleries below.

A Ferris-wheel-type circulation loop picks up and discharges passengers at six different points inside the structure; from those points the visitor climbs or descends via stairs and escalators. In addition, there are two vertical elevator cores, primarily for freight and service personnel.

The structure of the two cantilevered volumes is an octahedral space frame, spanning 14 meters at each bay and providing a clear floor height of 5 meters and multiples or fractions of that dimension. The struts of the frame themselves were to be open-web, triangulated members, 80 centimeters in cross section, allowing all the electrical, mechanical, and ventilation services to be accommodated within the hollow struts.

38. Entry in the competition "Place Beaubourg," 1971.

39. Roof plan.

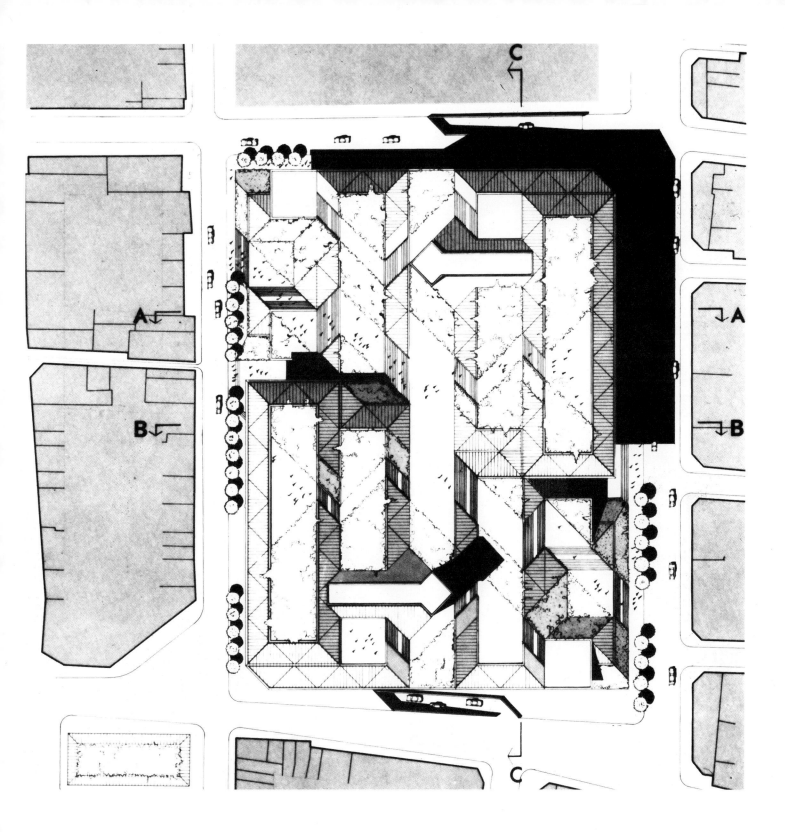

40. View of the complex from street level.

41. Axonometric view of the complex showing the "dish" with its surrounding service floors of parking and galleries, and the two inclined membranes above accommodating the library and museum.

**Meeting Places**
292-293
**Centre du Plateau Beaubourg**

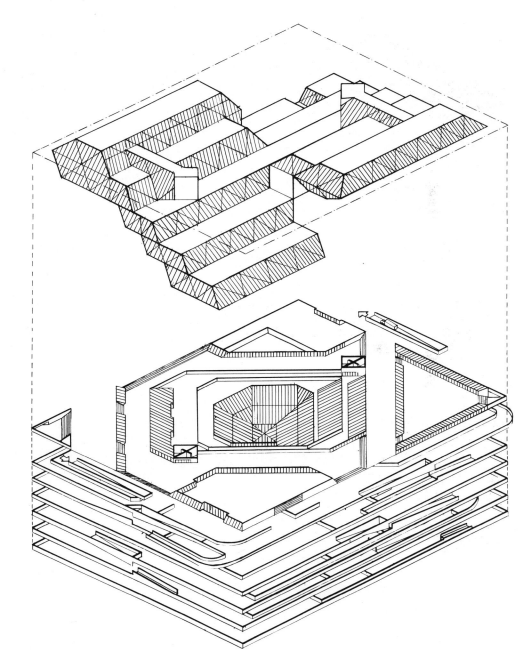

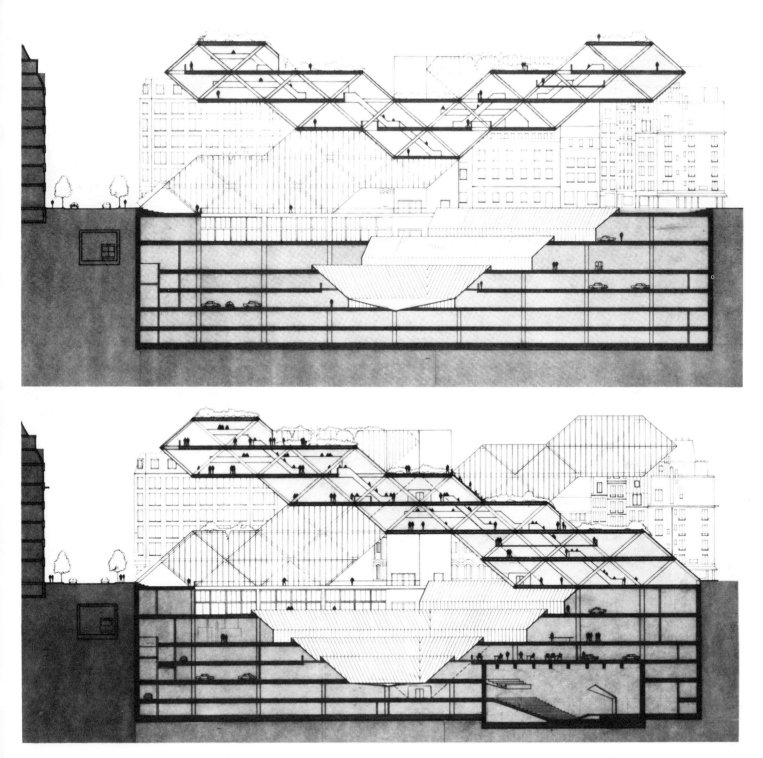

43, 44. Section.

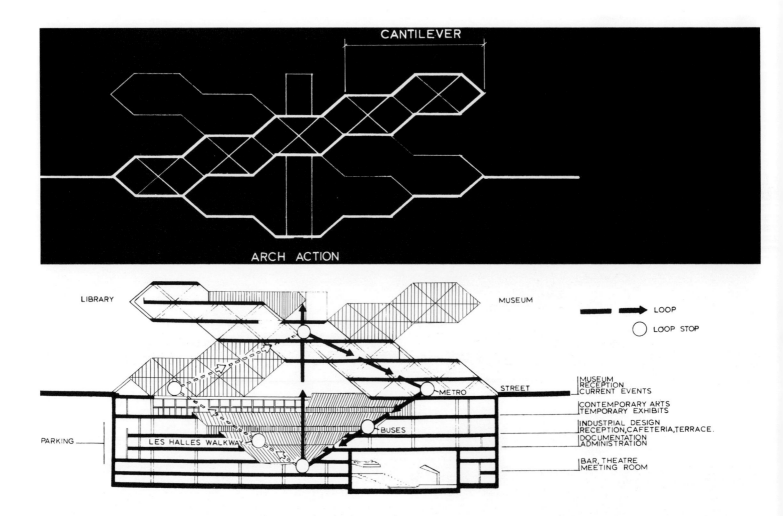

CANTILEVER

ARCH ACTION

LIBRARY

MUSEUM

LOOP

LOOP STOP

STREET

MUSEUM
RECEPTION
CURRENT EVENTS

CONTEMPORARY ARTS
TEMPORARY EXHIBITS

INDUSTRIAL DESIGN
RECEPTION, CAFETERIA, TERRACE.

DOCUMENTATION
ADMINISTRATION

BAR, THEATRE
MEETING ROOM

METRO

BUSES

PARKING

LES HALLES WALKWAY

45. The structural system.

46. The loop circulation system, linking entries from Les Halles, the Métro, the street levels, the library, and museums.

47. View from the north showing the cantilevered structure.

**Yeshivat Porat Joseph**
Yeshivat Porat Joseph, a Sephardic rabbinical college, is located in the Jewish Quarter of the Old City of Jerusalem, directly across the open plaza from the Western Wailing Wall; the yeshiva sits on the rock escarpment that rises 60 feet from the Western Wall Plaza.

48. View of the Old City from the Mount of Olives.
   A montage of the yeshiva is shown by the large building in the left side of the photograph, to the right of the white wall.

On the north side of the building are the new processional stairs recently constructed to connect the Jewish Quarter with the Wall; to the south, it is bounded by the ancient city wall built by Suliman the Magnificent which winds down to the Dung Gate.

Looking east, toward the Wall, one also sees the Temple Mount, the mosques of Omar and El Aksa, Mount Scopus and the Mount of Olives, and the Arab village of Siloam.

The yeshiva site was acquired at the turn of the century, one of the first to be purchased rather than leased by the Jewish residents of the Old City. The original yeshiva structure was built during the early part of the twentieth century, and was entirely destroyed in the 1948 Arab-Israeli war.

In 1967 the directors of the yeshiva decided to return to the original site, laying the cornerstone shortly after the Six Day War.

49. Aerial view of the Old City.

The yeshiva is a residential college. The students live in the institution and study toward rabbinical status. They range from the age of sixteen upwards. There are a number of categories of studies: the regular studies for single students; the "Kolel" studies for married students who do not live in the yeshiva; and the "mekubalim" studies, which are highly advanced explorations of the Scriptures by elders who have been duly qualified. The yeshiva consists of
- residences for two hundred and fifty students
- the Bait Midrash, the main study hall that also serves as a prayer hall and is the center of the life of the yeshiva students
- a series of classrooms of various sizes
- a library
- a physical health center, including a swimming pool and a gymnasium
- dining facilities for three hundred students and faculty
- social rooms and common rooms for students and faculty
- the administrative headquarters for the yeshiva
- an auditorium seating two hundred and fifty
- a youth synagogue
- a public synagogue (seating four hundred) that will function as one of the centers of the Sephardic Community.

The total floor area called for by the program is 140,000 square feet, to be located on a site approximately three-quarters of an acre in area.

The directors of the yeshiva expressed the desire that the synagogue chamber should be brightly colored as an expression of joyousness that they associated with the synagogue. The conventional use of stained glass was proposed, but I pointed out that this contradicted the tradition of "Thou shall not make thyself a graven image" and that it was basically a Christian concept. I therefore set out to seek some way in which color could be the result of a totally nonformal system. The solution proposed is for the light entering the synagogue chamber from the skylights to come through giant prisms. These prisms would break the sun's rays into a full spectrum of colors. The stone walls would then be flooded with an overlapping series of spectra that would change constantly with the position of the sun and with every passing cloud.

The synagogue chamber is thus formed as a room within a room. The precast elements rise six stories in height and are domed with translucent plastic. This lacy structure sits within the stone walls that contain passages and light shafts.

The studies take place primarily in the Bait Midrash. There the students work an average of eight hours per day and also undertake the three daily prayers. Students group in pairs or threes within the room, discuss and debate matters of interpretation of the Scriptures and refer to the teacher for advice when needed. There are approximately two hundred and fifty students in the room at any given time discussing the subject matter in high voice simultaneously.

The Bait Midrash has traditionally served as synagogue, and on holidays and Saturdays the public would participate in prayer with the students. In view of the location of the structure and the constant flow of pilgrims to the Western Wall, it was considered that this traditional arrangement would interfere excessively with the life of the yeshiva and it was therefore decided to provide a separate synagogue for public use.

The building rises ten stories from its eastern to its western side. The site is divided by an arcaded street separating the institution into uptown and downtown sections. Uptown are the residences and their related facilities: the dormitory rooms arch over a large space within which is the main dining room. Downtown are the academic facilities: the classroom, library, Bait Midrash, and the synagogue.

The Jerusalem bylaws demand that all exterior building surfaces, that is, both walls and roofs, be built of stone. From the outset, I tried to design the building in such a way that it would form a continuous whole with the rest of the Old City, but I nevertheless wanted to utilize contemporary building methods with all their potential. In order to resolve this dilemma, I chose a dual system for building. Ten-foot-thick, traditionally built stone walls enclose the site and define the major zones of the building.

The stone walls carry all the continuous linear and vertical services within the structure as well as all the passages, staircases, and light shafts. Within the spaces created by the stone walls is a second and completely contemporary construction system of precast concrete arch segment. The precast element, 10 feet high and 10 feet in horizontal reach, can form rooms 20 feet by 20 feet, 40 feet by 40 feet, 60 feet by 60 feet, 80 feet by 80 feet, and 100 feet by 100 feet. As the rooms become greater in area, they become higher.

51. View of the site from the Kotel Plaza.

52. Montage view.

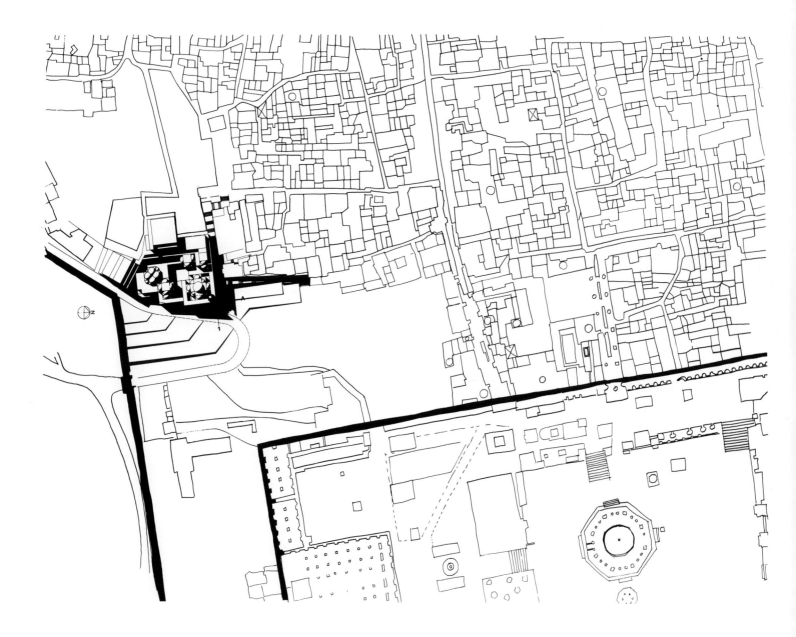

53. Site plan—Yeshivat Porat Joseph.

54-56. Sketches of the development of the
design for the yeshiva.

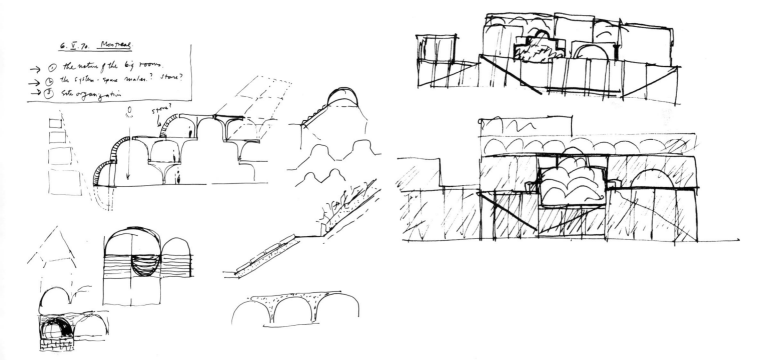

57. Sectional view of model showing relationship of stone and precast structures in
the synagogue and the northern entrance.

BAIT MIDRASH

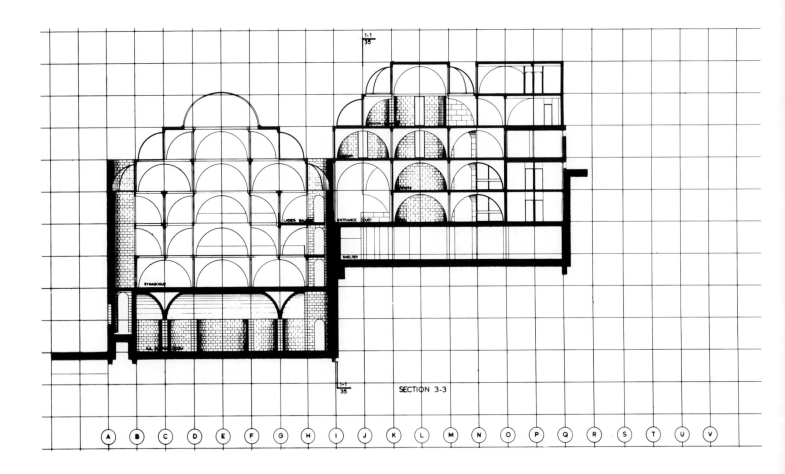

SECTION 3-3

59. Northwest section through the building showing the synagogue and women's galleries, entrance, offices, youth synagogue, and residences.

60. East-west section through the structure showing dining hall and residences, health complex and swimming pool, auditorium and classrooms.

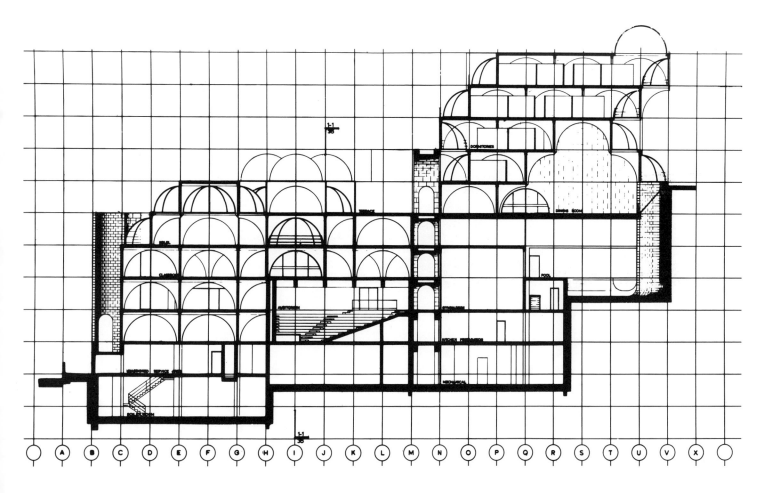

61. An assembly of the precast bents.

62, 63. Structural details.

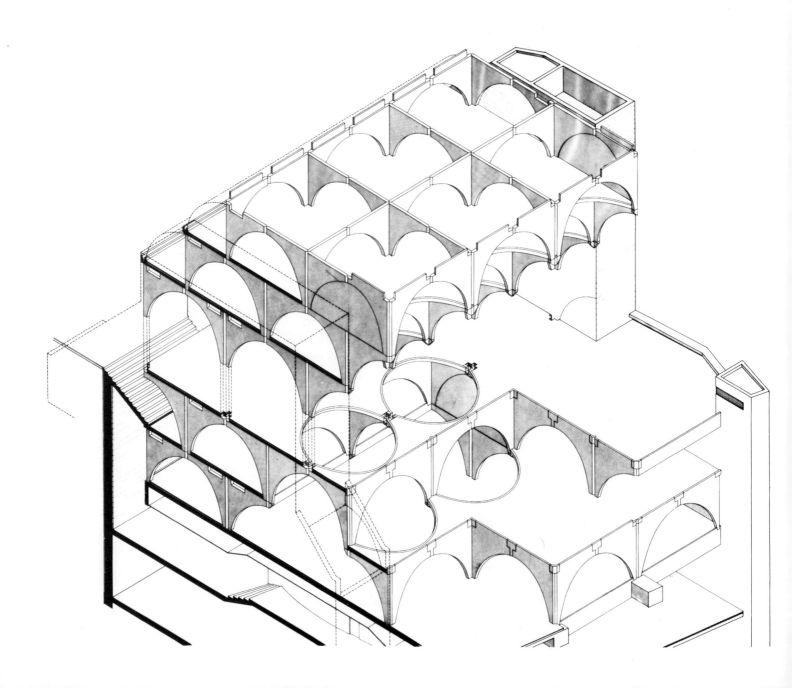

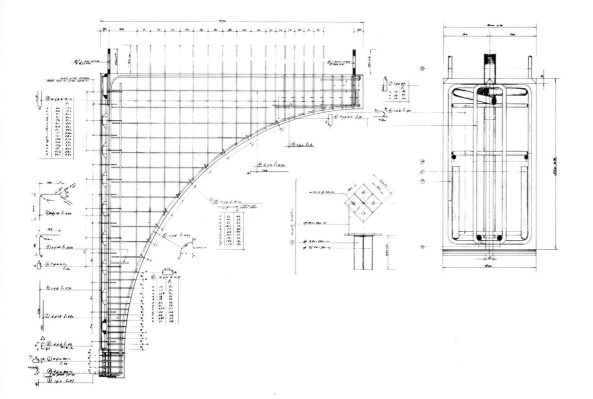
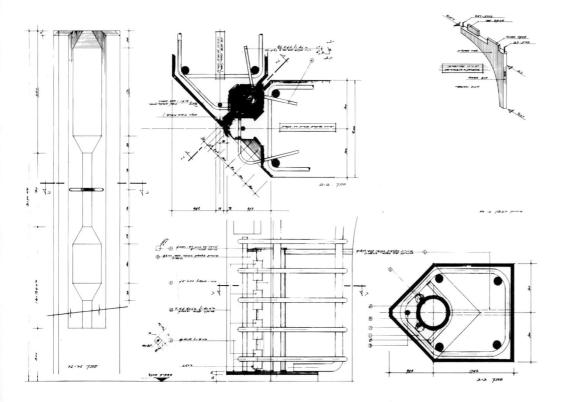

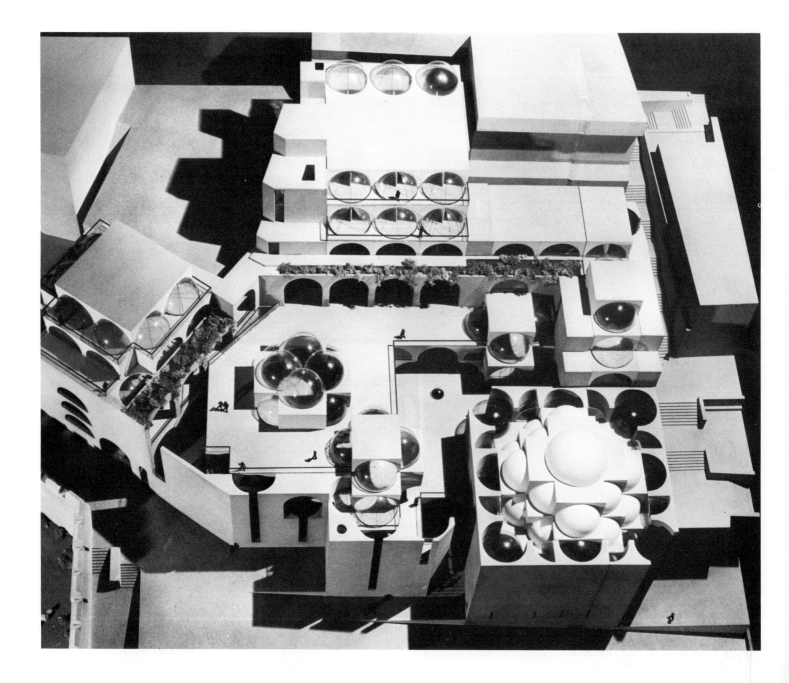

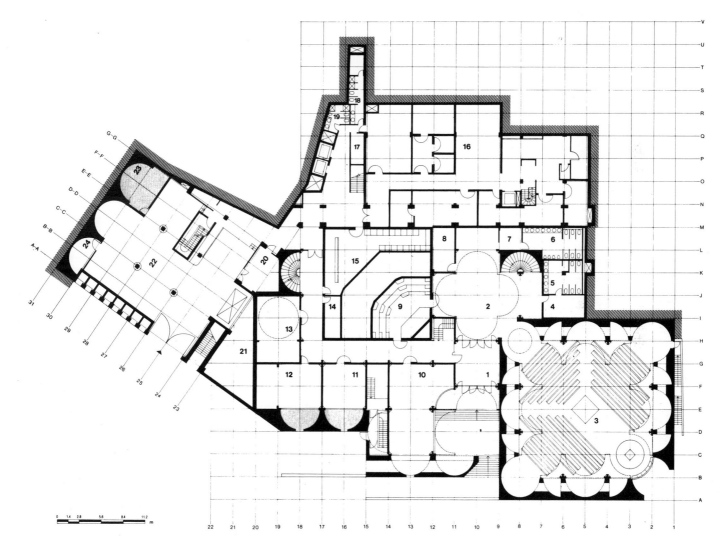

64. General view of the yeshiva.

65. Plan of the yeshiva at the main synagogue level.

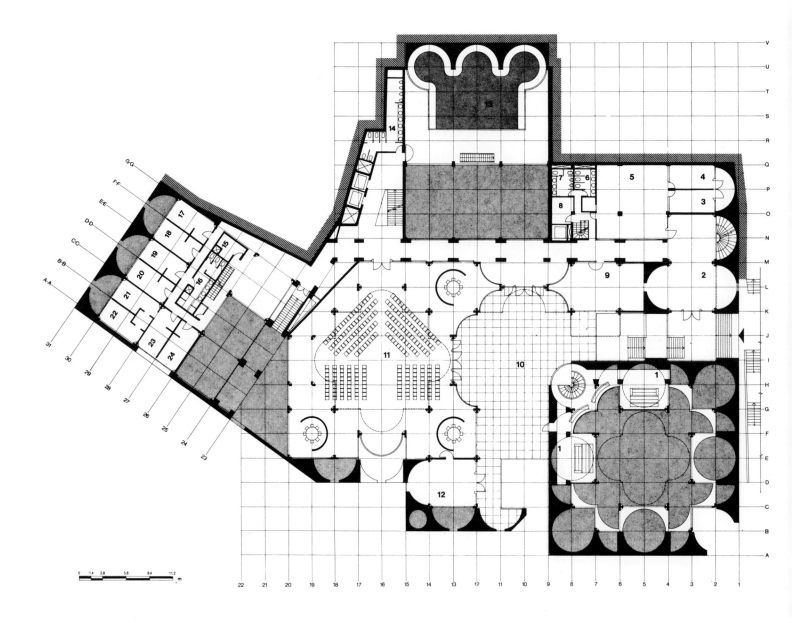

66. Plan of the yeshiva—Bait Midrash level.

67. Plan of the yeshiva—dining hall level.

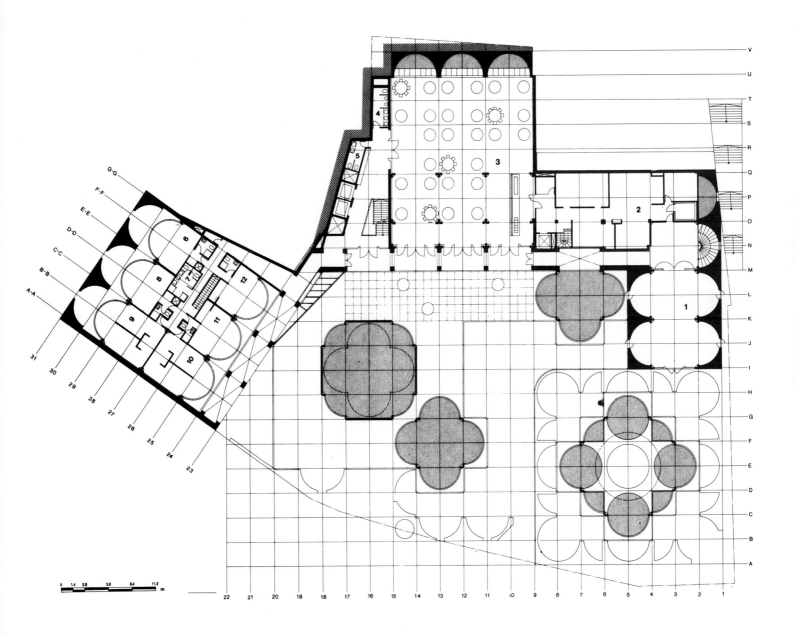

70. Interior of the synagogue.

71. Prisms break the light into a wash of
color.

72. Aerial view of the area of the Temple Mount and the Western Wall showing the space in front of the Wall which is to be reconstructed.

73. A mass protest meeting at the Western Wall.

## Western Wall Plaza

For me this problem became how to create a place where ten people can pray, three thousand can celebrate, and fifty thousand can demonstrate. Excavating to the original Herodian level seemed logical, since that would restore the Wall to its original scale, almost twice its present height. People, however, approach the area from many different elevations, and I felt that these various paths of movement should not be interrupted. So my proposals have taken an amphitheater form, with streets entering at several levels and space for important public institutions on the periphery, the crown of the amphitheater. Parts of the amphitheater are broad and open, parts form a narrow and quite intimate space close to the Wall.

The amphitheater forms a series of piazzas ascending from the Herodian street adjacent to the Western Wall ten stories up to the level of the Jewish Quarter with the small houses poised on the cliff overlooking the Temple Mount. Adjacent to the Wall we have the palatial scale of large public places defined by large structures, and, as we move away from it and upwards, the public spaces become smaller and we come to the scale of the small cubes and domes of the houses, 5 or 6 meters in width. The problem was to establish a building vocabulary that could transform in scale from the palatial to the residential, from the public to the private: piazzas 25 meters in width transforming to covered streets 12 meters in width, transforming gradually to the scale of the houses on the cliff, a sliding geometric scale of small to large places, of small to large surfaces.

The geometry has an added level of complexity inasmuch as I was convinced that, as in the yeshiva of Porat Joseph, there was a need to have a hierarchy of the prime spaces and service spaces adjacent to them. These service spaces would form the circulation and distribution within the buildings and the ramp and the stairs within the piazzas. But the service space of the large area had to vary proportionally to that of the service space of a small area. At the same time, the basic geometry of the building component should be capable of vertical stacking in section (a spiraling vertical space) or horizontal grouping in plan. This developed into a building vocabulary that can make scale transition in plan and in section and can answer the multitude of spatial requirements of the piazzas and the surrounding buildings within an ordered system. The system generates both piazzas and buildings, so that the amphitheater is an integration of outdoor and indoor spaces, without a clear separation line between piazzas and the surrounding buildings.

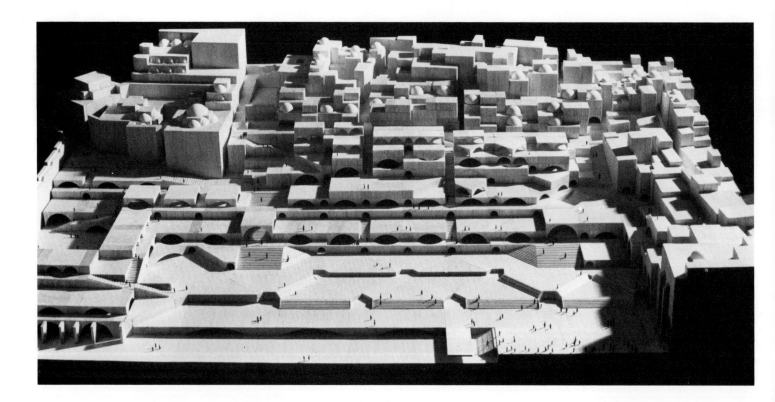

74. View to the west of the piazzas, the arcaded street, the public buildings, Yeshivat Porat Joseph, and the residences of the Jewish Quarter with the praying area adjacent to the Wall in the foreground.

75. Diagram showing the geometry and construction method for the project. The scale of the element varies from the public scale (Unit A) to the smallest residential scale (Unit E). The service spaces between the elements vary in size with the spaces which they are serving. Scale transition from the largest to the smallest is possible in plan as one moves from the Wall to the residential area or vertically as the heights of the buildings increase.

**Meeting Places**
322-323
**Plaza by the Western Wall**
**Hierarchical Generative System**

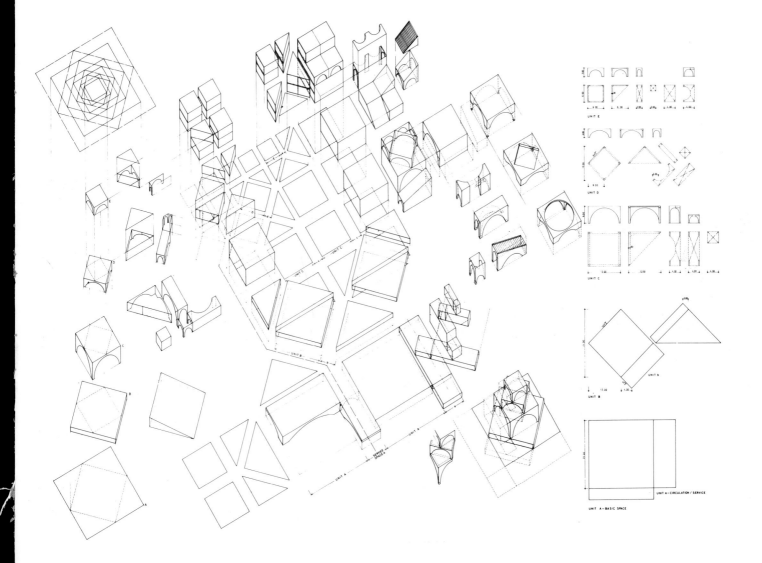

76. Axonometric view of the piazza. Note at
the bottom that the terraced piazzas con-
tinue southeast toward David City forming
an archaeological amphitheater. The upper
levels (wall structure) are restorations of
buildings of the Omayyad Muslim period
(from A.D. 660 on). The other levels will
contain restorations of Crusader, Byzantine,
and Herodian periods.

77. Pedestrian movement throughout the piazza showing connections to Dung Gate, the Jewish Quarter, the markets, the Temple Mount, and movement within the piazza itself.

78. General view of the area showing the terraced piazzas ascending from the Herodian
street level adjacent to the Wall up to the level of the Jewish Quarter. Public institutions
form the crown of the ascending piazzas
with the Rabbinical High Court located to
the north and Yeshivat Porat Joseph being
the building to the south. A small square
forms an anteroom by Dung Gate (lower
left) leading to an arcaded street that crosses
the piazza and connects it to the markets on
the north.

79. View of the piazzas from Dung Gate showing, in the center of the Western Wall, Barkley's Gate (one of the original Herodian entrances to the Temple) which would be exposed when the area is excavated to its original Herodian level.

80. Detail of the praying piazza adjacent to the Western Wall. The bridge at bottom right leads to the unearthed Barkley's Gate. The arcade in the foreground leads to the underground chambers of the Herodian and later periods.

In the design of the Kotel Plaza, the area in front of the Western Wall in Jerusalem, we are dealing with a site that has been a meeting place for thousands of years—a pilgrimage place. Over the centuries, it has undergone several transformations of scale. The Wall is the remaining fragment of the retaining wall that enclosed and supported the second Temple constructed by Herod and destroyed by Titus. Two hundred years ago, the space in front of the Wall, which was encroached upon by later construction, was only 20 feet wide and about 200 or 300 feet long. Perhaps at any one time, it could have accommodated two hundred people. Entry to the area was through a very narrow alley of stairs; it was really like a roofless room. People used it like a synagogue without a roof.

About a hundred years ago, several Jews bought some properties and managed to demolish them and widen the space, so that it became 40 feet deep. But it was still a roofless room. I can remember it that way from a visit as a child in 1947. Because the space was so small, the Wall and the stones in it looked quite enormous. Then in 1967, when the Six Day War was over, by a mysterious decision that's very hard to trace, the bulldozers moved in before anyone had a chance to breathe, and they cleared a space that is 400 or 500 feet wide and 1000 feet long. They cleared the entire mass of buildings in front of the Wall, and they stopped almost arbitrarily at the cliff of rocks that divides the upper and the lower city. The space that was created by the bulldozers is the same size as the Piazza San Marco in Venice. Now the Wall looks like a little fence. But on Saturday nights there may be ten thousand people there. On High Holidays there are perhaps forty thousand. During a march to express sympathy for the Russian Jews there were eighty thousand people. But, in spite of that, it really isn't a meeting place. In fact, it looks like the preparation for a parking lot.

After being commissioned to consider the design for the area, I first started sketching plazas, paving this great area with stone, I began to wonder what it would feel like to come in the evening and pray there with four or five other people, on the edge of a flat plaza that extends 500 feet in one direction and 1000 feet in another. Wouldn't you feel exposed, lonely, and unsheltered? Wouldn't the intimacy of praying by the Wall that existed there for thousands of years be destroyed? And if praying by the Wall is equated with the quality of praying in a synagogue, then surely, if you were not praying, you would feel terribly uncomfortable just strolling past those who were. At present, there is a little fence, with a man who guards it and gives you a cap to put on your head if you want to come inside the place of prayer.

So for me the problem became how to create a place where ten people can pray, three thousand can celebrate, and fifty thousand can demonstrate. Excavating to the original Herodian level seemed logical, since that would restore the Wall to its original scale, almost twice its present height. People, however, approach the area from many different elevations, and I felt that these various paths of movement should not be interrupted. So my later sketches have taken an amphitheater form, with streets entering at several levels and space for important public institutions on the periphery. Parts of the amphitheater are broad and open, parts form a narrow and quite intimate space close to the wall. I am hopeful that this will be tied back into the existing city with appropriate scale and many paths of pedestrian movement.

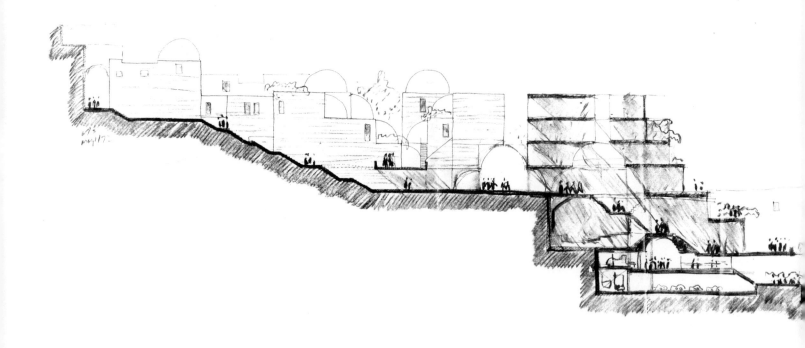

Shortly after I was commissioned to work on the Western Wall Plaza, I went down there, at sunset, on the eve of a holiday. Thousands were streaming through for prayer. As the prayer commenced, the chant of the Muezzin calling the Moslems to prayer on the Temple mount intermingled with the sound of the praying Jews. A procession of Franciscan priests in brown robes crossed the plaza to watch the Jews in prayer. Then simultaneously, the bells of the churches in the Christian quarter began to chime. To the west were the terraced and domed residences of the Jewish quarter; to the east, the palatial walls of Herod's Temple and the Moslem mosques above them; to the south, the Turkish city walls of Sultan Suliman the Magnificent. Places for living and worship on the scale of a house, a temple, and a palace.

Can one create a contemporary vernacular and reestablish the basic values of this environment? Can one build continuity from the old to the new? Can one unite the scales of all life's activities? It seemed, there in Jerusalem—the city of all men, a place of holiness, of deep love and longing—that the process of mending its scars and restoring its vitality might be the fulfillment of a dream of reconciliation for all mankind.

# CREDITS

## Habitat 67
**Original Scheme**

Architect:
Moshe Safdie, Architect

Structural Consultant:
Dr. A. Komendant

Client:
Canadian Corporation for the
1967 World Exhibition

Photographs:
Arnott Rogers

## Habitat 67

Architect:
Moshe Safdie and David, Barott, Boulva,
Associated Architects

Structural Consultant:
Dr. A. Komendant

Consulting Engineers:
Monti, Lefebvre, Lavoie,
Nadon & Associates

Mechanical and Electrical Engineers:
Huza Thibault and
Nicolas Fodor & Associates

Landscape Consultants:
Harper-Lantzius Consortium

Client:
Canadian Corporation for the
1967 World Exhibition

Photographs:
Keith Oliver, Jerry Spearman

## New York Habitat I
## and
## New York Habitat II

Architect:
Moshe Safdie, Architect

Structural Engineers:
Conrad Engineers and T. Y. Lin & Associates

Client:
Carol Haussamen Foundation, New York

Photographs:
Moshe Safdie, Architect

## Puerto Rico Habitat

Architect:
Moshe Safdie, Architect

Structural Engineers:
Conrad Engineers

Mechanical and Electrical Engineers:
Dickerson/Gladstone Associates

Associated Architect (Puerto Rico):
R. A. Perez-Marchand & George Z. Mark

Associated Structural Engineer
(Puerto Rico):
Hugh A. C. Martin

Associated Mechanical, Electrical, and
Plumbing Engineers (Puerto Rico):
Ibarra Garcia, Firpi & Villaneuva,
Rodriguez Olivieri

Client:
Development International Corporation

Photographs:
Jerry Spearman

Sketch of Factory:
Bruce Johnson

## Tropaco

Architect:
Moshe Safdie, Architect

Structural Engineers:
Conrad Engineers

Client:
Armour Enterprises, St. Thomas,
U.S. Virgin Islands

Photographs:
Jerry Spearman

## Indian Carry
**Saranac Lake**

Architect:
Moshe Safdie, Architect

Structural Engineers:
Baracs & Gunter

Mechanical and Electrical Engineers:
Huza Thibault

Client:
Indian Carry Associates

Photographs:
Moshe Safdie, Architect

## Israel Habitat

Architect:
Moshe Safdie, Architect

Structural Engineers:
Conrad Engineers and T. Y. Lin & Associates

Client:
Ministry of Housing, Government of Israel

**Rochester Habitat**

Architect:
Moshe Safdie/John Fujiwara, Architects

Structural Engineers:
Conrad Associates

Clients:
FIGHT/City of Rochester/New York Urban
Development Corporation

Photographs:
George Pollowy

**Coldspring New Town**

Architect:
Moshe Safdie & Associates

Development Consultants:
Rouse-Wates, Incorporated

Landscape Architects:
Lawrence Halprin & Associates

Economic Consultants:
Gladstone Associates

Structural and Service Engineering
Consultants:
Conrad Associates

Cost Estimating Consultants:
Robert Hughes Associates

Transportation Consultants:
DeLeuw, Cather & Associates

Client:
The City of Baltimore acting through the
Department of Housing and Community
Development, Baltimore, Maryland

Photographs:
Martin Hoffmeister and
Moshe Safdie & Associates

**College Union**
**San Francisco State College**

Architects:
Moshe Safdie and Burger & Coplans
Associated Architects

Structural Engineers:
Conrad Engineers

Mechanical and Electrical Engineers:
Huza Thibault with Hanson & Peterson

Food Service Consultants:
Bernard & Associates with
Laschober & Sovich Inc.

Client:
College Union Council, San Francisco
State College

**Paris Competition**

Architect:
Moshe Safdie, Architect

Project Team:
Heather Willson Cass, Roberta Lawrence,
Martin Hoffmeister, Deborah Lee,
Clinton Sheerr, James Strickland,
Robert Yudell, Henry Wollman

Photographs:
Jerry Spearman and Martin Hoffmeister

**Yeshivat Porat Joseph**

Architect:
Moshe Safdie, Architect

Associated Architect:
David Best

Structural Engineers:
Lev Zetlin Associates, Inc.

Mechanical Engineers:
A. Yosha, A. Schwartz, U. Greenbaum

Electrical Engineers:
A. Guilad & Co.

Lighting Consultants:
Wheel Garon Inc.

Acoustic Consultants:
Bolt Beranek and Newman Inc.

Quantity Surveyors:
D. Shaviv

Project Managers:
Dov Levitt Assoc.

Contributing Artist on Prism Lighting:
Charles Ross

Client:
The World Committee for Reconstruction
of Yeshivat Porat Joseph

Photographs:
Charles Ross and Moshe Safdie & Associates

**Factory Feasibility Study**

Consultants:
Conrad Engineers

**Kotel**
**Western Wall Plaza**

Architect:
Moshe Sfadie, Architect

Client:
The Corporation for the Development of
the Jewish Quarter and the City of Jerusalem

# INDEX